SUNDIALS

Other reissues by SPCK

English Churchyard Memorials Frederick Burgess
English Mediaeval Painted Glass J. D. Le Couteur

SUNDIALS
Incised Dials or Mass-Clocks

A Study of the Time-Markers of
Medieval Churches, Containing
Descriptions, Photographs, Diagrams,
and Analysis of Dials,
Chiefly in Hampshire,
But Also in Various Other Counties

ARTHUR ROBERT GREEN
MRCS ENGLAND, LRCP LONDON

LONDON
SPCK

First published in the Historic Monuments of England series 1926
First paperback edition 1978
SPCK
Holy Trinity Church
Marylebone Road
London NW1 4DU

Printed in Great Britain by
Whitstable Litho Ltd., Millstrood Road, Whitstable, Kent.

ISBN 0 281 03656 X

DEDICATED TO

A. M. J.

FOREWORD

THE author of this book has asked me to supply a brief foreword to his study of a subject which hitherto only one or two writers have thought worthy of attention. The frequent occurrence of small dials cut in the outer walls of churches in all parts of England is a phenomenon well-known to ecclesiologists; but it is only of recent years that its practical object has been taken seriously into consideration. Among workers who have taken pains to tabulate examples in special districts, no one, so far as I am aware, has tested current theories by observation and comparison so thoroughly as Dr. Green. The scientific method by which he has arrived at his conclusions will be apparent to every reader of his volume. His researches remind us that there are still many points in the fabric and furniture of our churches which, small and unimportant as they may seem at first sight, deserve careful investigation on systematic lines. During the past quarter of a century there has been a great advance of intelligent curiosity with regard to ancient monuments, which can no longer be satisfied with haphazard conjectures; and such attempts as the present, undertaken in a circumscribed and almost untravelled field, illustrate the anxiety with which each detail of such monuments is being examined and compelled to render up its meaning. Work conceived in this spirit and with this end needs no apology, and its results may be heartily recommended to students and the general reader alike.

A. HAMILTON THOMPSON.

PREFACE

THE primitive time-markers which are the subject of this book are really sundials of an unscientific kind, and in order to distinguish them from every other variety of sundial they are generally mentioned here under the title of " Mass-clocks."

It seems a pity that hitherto so little interest has been taken in this subject, for it undoubtedly forms a very interesting corner in ecclesiology. To many people who take an intelligent interest in the architecture of our old parish churches the Mass-clock is quite unknown ; they will converse quite learnedly of the Norman, Early English, Decorated and Perpendicular styles of architecture, and they are interested in piers and arches, stained-glass windows, screens and pews, fonts, pulpits, bells, low side-windows and wall-paintings, etc., etc., but when one of these dials is mentioned, they have never seen or even heard of such a thing. Perhaps this may be accounted for in part by the deplorable habit so many people have of hurrying to inspect the inside of a church before they have mastered the details of the exterior.

Quite recently a lady wrote a letter to the *Morning Post* in which she deplored the fact that no one ever devises a new hobby. Well, here is an interesting, fascinating and inexpensive one—the collecting of photographs of and the study of Mass-clocks, and if it is not absolutely new, it is a hobby which at least is not overdone, and in these days when people are like a

ix

flock of sheep, and what one does all must do, that in itself is something for which to be thankful.

The great difficulty which presents itself in writing on a subject such as this, which is not easily explained, contains many debatable points, and inevitably involves some astronomical and mathematical considerations, is to strike the happy mean between too much detail and the presentation of facts so sparingly that the argument is obscure. It is hoped that by omitting many details of experimental work, by the use of the very numerous photographs and diagrams, and by the critical examination of the separate lines in the case of a number of dials, this difficulty has, at least in a great measure, been overcome. To the reader totally unacquainted with the subject the first three chapters should form a sufficient introduction. Subsequent chapters deal with some experimental work undertaken by the writer, and with a theory founded on this work which explains how it is possible for Mass-clocks to be real time-markers.

In connection with these experiments a conspectus of results may be useful.

A sundial marks the time by the shadow of its gnomon or style, which falls on the face of the dial when exposed to the rays of the sun.

No style belonging to a Mass-clock exists *in situ* at the present time, and so the shape of the style and the direction towards which it pointed when it stood out from the face of the dial is a matter of conjecture. The whole question resolves itself into this : Was the style straight or was it bent ? and if the latter, in what direction did the bent style point and what was the amount of the bending ?

The experiments prove that in order that the time should be accurately marked some Mass-clocks require to be fitted with a straight style for a portion of the year, but that generally, and for the vast majority, bent styles are required and that the bending is necessary in two directions, viz. they have to be bent downwards and they have to be bent also to one side so that they point directly due south.

Styles are thus seen to be of various kinds, and the special variety of style or styles necessary for a Mass-clock depends on the aspect of the wall on which it is incised, i.e. to what point of the compass it faces. These two points, the shape of the gnomon and the aspect of the dial, are thus of the utmost importance for the correct understanding of the functions of Mass-clocks ; but given a gnomon of the right shape and direction, the Mass-clock is a correct time-marker even when it faces to the east or the west of a due south aspect.

Throughout the first part of the book constant reference to the " Standard Dial " is necessary, and the reader would be wise to master thoroughly its very simple details.

Chapter VIII deals with the various theories which have been brought forward to explain these dials, and the conclusion which the writer has come to is that the Bent-Style Theory propounded in Chapter V offers the best explanation.

The analysis of dials has received considerable attention because of the necessity of proving that the position of lines on Mass-clocks follows a definite rule and that the angles they form are practically always 15 degrees apart or half 15 degrees or some multiple of $7\frac{1}{2}$ degrees.

By comparing the photograph, the diagram, the analysis and the description of a dial with the Standard Dial, a far fuller comprehension of all the details will be arrived at than can possibly be obtained by the most exhaustive inspection of the real dial as it exists on the church wall.

There then follow in Chapter X brief descriptions of all the dials which the writer has examined. This list will, it is believed, be appreciated by all those who take a keen interest in the subject, and it is only by the publication of such lists that our knowledge can be increased. The dials mentioned are chiefly drawn from Hampshire, but that is not a disadvantage, for their characteristics are the same all over the country, and in this case, what is true of one district holds good of another.

In this place I wish to offer my sincere thanks for much kind help. First of all my thanks are due to Mr. G. W. Willis and Mr. Ellaway, who most generously placed at my disposal the whole of their records and photos of dials in the neighbourhood of Basingstoke. Although all the churches on their list were visited and the dials photographed by myself, the value of the information received from them was much appreciated and the saving of time enormous. The survey of dials which they have made will, I hope, be published shortly in *The Proceedings of the Hants Field Club*.

I have received much kindly aid and advice from Mr. W. J. Andrew, F.S.A., and my thanks are given to him and to Mr. O. G. S. Crawford, F.S.A., for the loan of books, etc.

Especially I desire to express my indebtedness to my brother Captain J. G. Green, R.N., for much help on mathematical and astronomical details, without which much of this book could not have been written.

My thanks are also due to Mr. E. S. McEuan for the photos of dials in Hayling Island and for much kind assistance during my visit to that neighbourhood.

My indebtedness to Mr. John Humphreys, F.S.A., is very great. It was at his suggestion that I first took up the subject of Mass-clocks, and his help has always been most generously and ungrudgingly given to me.

Dom Ethelbert Horne has most unselfishly allowed me to photograph and reproduce the stumps of two styles extracted from their style-holes and now in his possession, for which I am very grateful.

I am also indebted to Colonel E. M. Jack for information on the subject of " broad arrows."

Obligations are also acknowledged to other friends and correspondents too numerous to mention.

To Professor A. Hamilton Thompson I am particularly indebted for a variety of helpful suggestions, and I should also like to include my publishers, the Society for Promoting Christian Knowledge, in my grateful acknowledgments.

ARTHUR ROBERT GREEN.

CROYLAND, NEAR ROMSEY, HANTS.

BIBLIOGRAPHY

A History of Hampshire and the Isle of Wight. The Victoria History of the Counties of England. 5 Vols.

Primitive Sun Dials or Scratch Dials. Dom Ethelbert Horne, F.S.A.

"Yorkshire Dials," a paper in *The Yorkshire Archœological and Topographical Journal,* Parts XVII and XVIII. The Rev. Daniel Henry Haigh.

An unpublished lecture by Mr. George F. J. Rosenberg.

The Arts in Early England. Vol. II. *Anglo-Saxon Architecture.* New Edition, 1925.

The Arts in Early England. Vol. V. *The Ruthwell and Bewcastle Crosses, the Gospels of Lindisfarne and other Christian Monuments of Northumbria.*

The Arts in Early England. Vol. I. The *Life of Saxon England in its Relation to the Arts.* Professor G. Baldwin Brown, M.A.

Gothic Architecture. Thomas Rickman, F.S.A.

"Sundials," a paper in *The Antiquary,* Vol. XLIV. Alfred C. Fryer, Ph.D., F.S.A.

Book of Sundials. Mrs. Gatty.

"Weaverthorpe Church," *Archœologia,* Vol. LXXII. Mr. John Bilson, F.S.A.

Churchwardens' Accounts. The Rev. J. Charles Cox.

Encyclopœdia Britannica.

The English Parish Church. 1914. The Rev. J. Charles Cox.

The Cathedral Churches of England. 1925. Professor A. Hamilton Thompson, M.A., F.S.A.

CONTENTS

CHAPTER I

TYPES OF DIALS

THE PURPOSE OF THE BOOK. VARIOUS DESIGNATIONS. THE TERM "MASS-CLOCK." LITERATURE ON THE SUBJECT. DOM ETHELBERT HORNE'S BOOK. HAIGH'S PAPER. MR. ROSENBERG'S LECTURE. HISTORICAL SURVEY. ROMAN DIALS IN ENGLAND. SAXON DIALS

CHAPTER II

SAXON SUNDIALS AND LATER TIME-MARKERS

SAXON SUNDIALS, KIRKDALE, EDSTON, WEAVERTHORPE, ESCOMBE, WARNFORD, CORHAMPTON, WINCHESTER, CASTLE FROOME, DAGLINGWORTH. THE DÆG-MÆL POINT. THE SAXON TIDES, THE TIDE-ANNOUNCER, THE NORMAN CONQUEST AND THE INTRODUCTION OF MASS-CLOCKS. THE ONLY KNOWN TIME-MARKERS FROM THE CONQUEST TO THE INTRODUCTION OF CLOCKS. DATE OF MASS-CLOCKS. CLOCKS. RING-DIALS. SCIENTIFICALLY CONSTRUCTED SUNDIALS. A GLASS SUNDIAL. TIME AT NIGHT AND ON SUNLESS DAYS, CANONICAL HOURS. DAY-BELL. MORROW-MASS. CRESSET-STONES

CHAPTER III

DESCRIPTION OF MASS-CLOCKS

DESCRIPTION OF MASS-CLOCKS. THE STYLE-HOLE. THE GNOMON OR STYLE. LINES. WHEEL-DIALS. HALF- AND QUARTER-WHEEL DIALS. HOLES. REVERSED DIALS. WHERE TO LOOK FOR MASS-CLOCKS. "COPY-DIALS." MULTIPLE DIALS. MOVABLE STYLES. THE "BROAD ARROW."

CONTENTS

LIST OF ILLUSTRATIONS

PHOTOGRAPHS, Half-tone

BETWEEN PAGES 140 AND 141

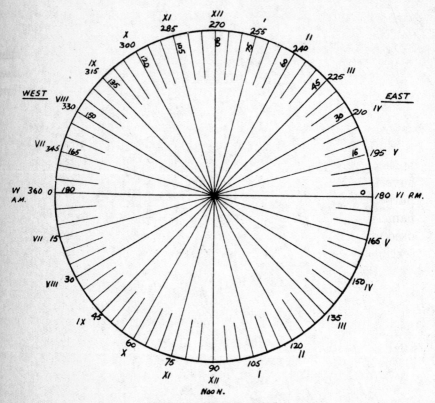

THE STANDARD DIAL.

The long lines are 15 degrees apart and mark the hours.
The short lines are 5 degrees apart and the intervals equal
20 minutes.

SUNDIALS

CHAPTER I
TYPES OF DIALS

THE purpose of this book is to bring to the reader's notice some facts about those insignificant and seldom observed marks which may be found incised on the walls of many of our ancient parish churches.

These marks—sometimes they are lines, sometimes holes, and often a combination of lines and holes—have been supposed in the past to have served various purposes and in consequence have been called by various names, but now almost everyone agrees that they were used as time-markers, either to mark the time when the service of Mass was said, when the term " Mass-clock " seems an appropriate one, or in addition to this, to point out the exact time when noon occurred, or to mark many or all of the hours between sunrise and sunset. Among the various designations (omitting such fanciful names as " sexton's wheel," " mason's mark," etc., etc.) may be mentioned " sundials," " primitive sundials," " incised sundials," " scratch dials," etc., and all of these terms are apt to be misleading, for by a dial or sundial on a church the " man in the street " immediately jumps to the conclusion that what is meant is one of those scientifically constructed dials which were so commonly placed on churches in the late seventeenth and eighteenth centuries. The dials now under consideration are much simpler than these and required in their making no scientific knowledge.

1

The two kinds are, in fact, entirely different, although superficially somewhat alike, and it would be advantageous if a term could be found to distinguish the simpler and earlier instrument from the later, and scientifically made sundial.

There are, of course, objections to the term " Mass-clock," the chief of which is that these dials generally did more than mark the time when Mass was said, and the word " clock " may also be objected to, for by its derivation it should be a contrivance which " strikes," but by common usage it has come to apply also to a machine for measuring time which marks the time by the position of its " hands " upon a dial plate.   The dials under consideration, however, measured the time and marked it in much the same manner by the use of a shadow instead of the " hands."   The word " clock " is also used with a similar meaning in the term " water-clock," and taking everything into consideration " Mass-clocks " or " primitive or medieval time-markers " seem to be the terms which describe them best.   That they did mark the time in nearly the same manner in which a clock does, although to a limited extent, will be fully demonstrated in later chapters, and in doing this the time for the service of Mass was also fixed ; indeed, the fixing of the time for this important service was probably their chief duty, but this did not prevent them from being of use in marking other hours of the day and especially perhaps noon.

Notwithstanding the objection mentioned above, the word " sundials " has been so commonly applied to these " sun-markers " (to use the old Saxon designation) that it has been thought best to retain it as the principal title of this book, and it is hoped that the sub-titles " Incised Dials or Mass-clocks " and " The Time-markers of Medieval Churches," will be sufficient to make it clear that the scientifically constructed sundial is not under consideration.

The term " Mass-clock " is not new ; indeed, in some parts of England it seems to be the one generally used, and as it is short and convenient it will be often employed in what is to follow.

It was during a visit to the Cotswolds that the writer's attention was first directed to this subject. About fifty churches were visited and no fewer than thirty-five Mass-clocks were found. Sometimes a church would only have a single dial, but one church was observed to have seven, and another six, and several churches possessed two. Curiosity was at once aroused. For what purpose were they made ? And if they were for the purpose of telling the time or for marking the church services, how did they perform those offices and were they accurate ? Naturally information was sought in any literature, but very little was found to have been written on this subject ; in fact, there appears to be only one book dealing with these dials. This book is entitled *Primitive Sun Dials or Scratch Dials*, and was written by Dom Ethelbert Horne, of Downside Abbey, near Bath. It contains a description of more than two hundred dials on Somerset churches, and is a most interesting book and one which anyone seeking information on the subject will find indispensable. Constant references to this work of Fr. Horne's will be found in subsequent pages.

A day spent at the British Museum yielded no information. The authorities there were most kind and innumerable catalogues and indices and books were explored, but not one single reference to the subject could be found.

There is a rather more abundant literature on dials of the Saxon period, but these, though at first sight rather similar, are really of a quite distinct type. Anyone interested in Anglo-Saxon dials may be referred to a most scholarly and interesting paper on " Yorkshire Dials " by the late Rev. Daniel Henry Haigh, published in *The Yorkshire Archæological and Topographical Journal.* This paper will often be quoted, especially in the section dealing with Saxon dials.

Mr. Rosenberg, in an unpublished lecture delivered to the Canterbury Archæological Society, has brought forward some new ideas as to the meaning of some of the lines on Mass-clocks. His theory will be discussed in some detail in a subsequent chapter.

Before a description of these dials is entered upon, and some experiments, tending to show how they can be made to tell the various hours, described, it may be interesting to make an historical survey of what is known as to the measurement of time in bygone ages.

Probably all the ancient civilizations such as the Egyptian, Minoan, Mesopotamian and Chinese possessed methods for measuring and marking time, and it would be interesting to know whether the methods used in later times have been derived from them. Very little, however, is known about the measurement of time in these very early civilizations ; but coming to a later period, in the first chapter of the Bible [1] we read, " And the evening and the morning were the first day," or as it is otherwise rendered, " And there was evening and there was morning, one day." From this we can gather that the Jews' day commenced in the evening.

The day was also divided into four parts [2] and the night into watches. [3]

Some easy method of dividing and measuring the parts of the day must have been recognized as a necessity in quite early times, and it has been surmised that the

[1] Gen. i. 5.   [2] Neh. ix. 3.   [3] 1 Sam. xi. 11, and Mat. xiv. 25.

first sundials may have been the invention of some Chaldean shepherd, who stuck his staff into the soil and marked by stones the progressive shadows of the sun's day.

Be this as it may, we have an early historical instance of a sundial in the dial of Ahaz,[1] who reigned over Judah from 741 B.C. to 725 B.C.

In 2 Kings xx. we read that Hezekiah, the son of Ahaz, was sick unto death, and the Lord sent Isaiah to tell him that he would die. Then Hezekiah prayed, and the Lord heard his prayer and told Isaiah to return to him and tell him that he would be healed. And Hezekiah said to Isaiah, " What shall be the sign that the Lord will heal me ? " Isaiah said, " This sign shalt thou have . . . shall the shadow go forward ten degrees, or go back ten degrees ? " Hezekiah chose that the shadow should return backward. And the Lord " brought the shadow ten degrees backward, by which it had gone down in the dial of Ahaz."

There have been many guesses respecting this dial of Ahaz, but it was most likely an obelisk approached by steps, down which the shadow would creep as the sun sank.

Two hundred years after the time of Ahaz our next historical sundial appears in Greece, and we find Diogenes asserting that Anaximander of Miletus invented the gnomon. This was probably a vertical rod on a horizontal plane, and the measurement of the shadow would enable observers to determine the solstices (the longest and shortest days) by its longest and shortest shadows at noon. This instrument by the shortest shadow in the day would mark noon or midday, and when the shadows at sunrise and sunset made a line at right angles to the noon-line, it would show the equinoxes. It would

[1] 2 Kings xx. 11.

not divide the day otherwise than into forenoon and afternoon.

The earliest sundial of which we have any certain knowledge is the " hemi-cycle " or hemisphere of the Chaldean astronomer Berosus, who lived probably about 340 B.C. This was a hollow hemisphere, fixed with its rim perfectly horizontal and having a bead or globule fixed at its centre. The shadow of this bead, as it moved during the day, was marked on the inside of the instrument, and this was done at various periods throughout the year. The line thus formed was divided into twelve equal parts, and in this way the day from sunrise to sunset was divided into twelve equal parts. These parts or hours were, however, not of equal length, the winter hours being short and the summer hours long.

The dial of Berosus remained in use for centuries and four specimens have been found in Italy, one of which was unearthed at Pompeii in 1762.

The Romans were neither great geometers nor astronomers, but they had dials which they obtained from the Greeks and these dials also divided the day into equal portions. Papirius Cursor placed a sundial in the court of the Temple of Quirinus in the year 293 B.C. Before this date noon was proclaimed by a crier when the sun appeared between the Rostra and a spot called the " station of the Greeks."

However, during the first Punic War a sundial was captured by Valerius Messalla at Catania in Sicily. This dial was set up in the Forum about 263 B.C., yet not having been calculated for the latitude of Rome, it told the time inaccurately for a hundred years.

During the whole of this time the hours were of unequal length and the use of equinoctial hours of uniform length did not come into common use until the fourth century of our era.

No account of the measurement of time would be complete if it did not mention the Clepsydra, or water-clock of the Greeks and Romans, but this of course does not depend on the shadow cast by the sun.

The measurement of time by water is a very ancient device, and just one example may be given here, namely, one which was constructed to show the intervals of the night, but generally they were made to show the periods of the day or of both the day and the night. The Clepsydra in question is shaped like a very large flower-pot and the outside is covered by hieroglyphics. It was found at Karnac Temple, Upper Egypt, and dates from the reign of King Amenhotep III, 1415–1380 B.C. There is a cast of it in the Victoria and Albert Museum.

On the inside of the vase are twelve scales, marked by dots, each scale being divided into ten parts corresponding with the month, of which the name is inscribed on the rim above the scale. The vessel was filled with water, which escaped slowly through a hole near the base, so that the water-level fell by one interval of the scale for each " hour " interval of the night. The scales for the winter months are longer, in order to allow for the period between sunset and sunrise being longer than in the months near the summer solstice.

Among the more curious methods used for the measurement of time the moon-dial may be mentioned. In one of the courts of Queen's College, Cambridge, there is a sundial which has around it a series of numbers to make it available as a moon-dial when the moon's age is known.

Another plan for the measurement of time was that in use in Iceland about a thousand years ago, and no doubt a survival from the principles of our stone circles. The method was to use the natural horizon of each township divided into eight equal parts, by mountain peaks or by pyramids of stone where natural marks were wanting. The sun passing over these marks enabled a careful division of the day to be made.

When we reach the period of the Roman occupation of Britain, it would seem that the knowledge of dial construction had somewhat advanced. Our evidence

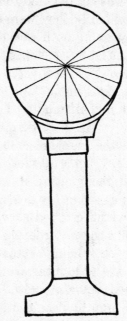

SKETCH OF DIAL FROM ROMAN PAVEMENT
AT BRADING, ISLE OF WIGHT.

of this is somewhat scanty, but the dial shown in the accompanying sketch seems to prove it, or at least to point in that direction. This representation of a dial (it is not a working dial) is to be seen on a tessellated pavement at the remains of a Roman villa at Morton, near Brading, Isle of Wight.

The dial represented is evidently a horizontal one, and below the column on the pavement is a terrestrial globe. Standing by the side is the figure of a man who holds a wand with which he points to the globe, and below is a pestle and mortar. These instruments are generally used to indicate a philosopher or man of science.[1] The villa was in occupation in the third and fourth centuries, and the mosaic when seen by the writer in October 1925 was in an excellent state of preservation.

No style is shown on the mosaic, nor does there appear to be a style-hole, and there are twelve lines, not thirteen, but nevertheless the day would seem to be divided into twelve parts or hours.

There is also a piece of a broken Roman sundial preserved in the Museum at Chesters on the North Tyne. It was found at the station of Borcovicus on the Roman Wall, and, as shown in the sketch given in *The Arts of Early England*, vol. I, the lines on it divide the day into twelve parts. A hole for the style remains, and the dial was no doubt set up in a vertical position and used as a time-marker.

From these examples we may conclude that the Romans in England not only understood the construction of sundials but used them to tell the time by, and that the system which they used was the duodecimal, which divided the day-night into twenty-four hours.

Continuing our survey of the time-markers, we find that Ireland possessed dials in the seventh or eighth century, some of which are still to be seen ; they are on upright stone pillars and the lines on them divide the day into four parts.

The same octaval method of time-reckoning is seen on the Saxon dials which still remain in England, and some of these, for instance that at Escombe, Durham, belong to the seventh century (see p. 10).

In Saxon England there is distinct evidence, as seen

[1] Illustrated in Victoria County History, *Hants*, vol. I, p. 314.

on various dials to be mentioned subsequently, that
the two systems, the octaval and the duodecimal, were
in use side by side.

Take, for instance, the dial on Bewcastle Cross,

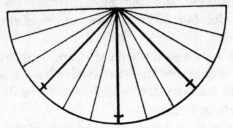

DIAGRAM OF DIAL ON BEWCASTLE CROSS; C. A.D. 675.

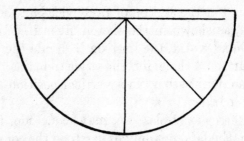

DIAGRAM OF DIAL AT ESCOMBE CHURCH, LATTER HALF
OF SEVENTH CENTURY.

Cumberland, which Professor Baldwin Brown dates at
about A.D. 675. It consists of the lower half of a circle
which is divided by radiating lines, each having a cross at
the end, into four equal parts, thus following the octaval
system. Each of these four parts is again divided into
three by two plain radiating lines. The whole half-circle
is thus divided into twelve parts, and so is in accordance
with the duodecimal system. The dial, if fitted with a
suitable gnomon, would thus tell the time according
to each system of reckoning, and it may have been, and
probably was, constructed for this purpose.

Those who have not seen the Bewcastle Cross can

examine the excellent cast of it in the Victoria and Albert Museum at South Kensington. From this it is clear that the lines marked with crosses are quite different from the plain lines, the former being deeper and wider and in section being more wedge- or V-shaped. There are several possible explanations of these differences. For instance, and this seems the most likely, the thirteen lines as they now appear may have been all incised at the same time in order to combine the Roman and the Saxon methods of time-marking; but it is also possible, though not perhaps probable, that the dial was at first what may be called a pure Saxon dial and divided the day into four parts by the deep, crossed lines, and at a later date the eight finer lines were added at a time when possibly the duodecimal system was more in vogue, i.e. after the Norman Conquest.

This dial on the Cross at Bewcastle is probably the most ancient Anglo-Saxon dial which has come down to us, but the one on Escombe Church, which is described on page 17, is of very nearly the same date.

In concluding this rapid and necessarily incomplete survey of the various devices and methods by which time was divided and measured before the Norman Conquest, it may be pointed out that the day-night has by various nations and at different periods been divided into 4 and 8, 6 and 12, 10 and 20, 12 and 24 parts. The earliest division was into four equal parts which later by halving each division gives us the octaval system, a system in use in different parts of India at the present time. Another method was to take the original four quarters and, dividing each into three parts instead of into two, thus to obtain twelve divisions for the day-night. This was again halved, giving us the duodecimal system now in common use. A decimal system of dividing time has also been used by some nations.

The consideration of the measurement of time in England from about the date of the Norman Conquest and for some centuries afterwards being the chief object in view in the writing of this book, it will be more convenient to leave that period for examination in later chapters. Clocks and scientifically constructed sundials will only receive a passing notice, but some reference to Greenwich time and the difference between it and sundial time will be necessary, and this subject will be dealt with in Chapter IV.

CHAPTER II

SAXON SUNDIALS AND LATER TIME-MARKERS

In various parts of England dials of pre-Conquest date are still to be found. They are remarkable for their excellent workmanship, and each is a definite piece of sculpture and not merely a collection of incised lines. As to the date when they were made, most may be assigned to the tenth or the first half of the eleventh century, but others have been thought by competent observers to date from the seventh or eighth century.

The dial faces project and are generally carved on the face of a square or rectangular stone and are enclosed within a double circle. A leaf-like ornament is frequently found at each of the four corners, and in some cases the lower half only of the circle is represented. The radiating lines on the dial are placed at equal distances from each other and are so disposed that the day is divided into four equal parts or tides, and near the end of each line a cross-bar is cut upon it.

The Anglo-Saxons generally followed the octaval system of the division of time and divided the day-night into eight equal parts, but examples are to be found on dials which seem to suggest other systems, namely, the decimal and duodecimal.

One of the most remarkable of these Saxon dials is to be seen at Kirkdale, Yorks, and, from the inscription on it, its date can be ascertained within the limit of the ten years 1056–1066. The church at Kirkdale is a small edifice, mostly of a much later date than the Conquest, but the western doorway, now stopped, and the arch to the chancel are both very rude and may be considered portions of a pre-Conquest church. On the south side of this church, but not in its original position, is a stone measuring 7 feet in width and 2 feet in height. In the centre of this stone is the dial and on either side is the inscription.

THE SAXON DIAL AND INSCRIPTION AT KIRKDALE CHURCH, YORKS; C. 1064.

The dial is represented as a half-circle with a double line at the circumference and five lines, each with a cross on them, divide it into four equal parts, each of which is again subdivided into two equal portions by four other lines, shorter than the first and having no crosses on them. Carved on this part is: "✠ Dis is dæges solmerca æt ilcum tide ✠" ("This is the day's sun-marker at every tide") and "✠ and Hawarth me wrohte and Brand P.R.S.," which may be translated, "Hawarth made me and Brand, priests."

The inscription to the right and left of this dial is the longest extant of the Anglo-Saxon period and a most valuable example of the pure English of the eleventh century.

It may be read thus (the omitted letters being under-lined) ; " ✠ Orm Gamalsuna bohte Sanctus Gregorius Minster thonne hit wes æl tobrocan and tofalan and he hit let macan newan from grunde Christe and Sanctus Gregorius in Eadward dagum Cyning in Tosti dagum Eorl ✠," which may be translated : "Orm, son of Gamal, bought St. Gregory's Church, when it was all broken and fallen down, and he caused it to be made new from the ground, to Christ, and St. Gregory, in Eadward's days, the King, and in Tosti's days, the Earl."

Eadward the King was Edward the Confessor, who reigned from 1042 to 1066, and Tosti was the younger brother of Harold, and son of Godwin, Earl of the West-Saxons. On the death of Siward in 1056 he was made Earl of Northumberland, and was slain September 25, 1066, at Stamford Bridge: so that the date of the church and dial is limited within these ten years and may be set down as c. 1064.

Orm, the founder, is named in Domesday Book as holding the manor of Kirkby and many others under Hugh Fitzbaldric, and there is a further entry: "Ibi p'b'r et eccl'a " (" There are there a priest and a church ").

Haigh says : " Orm's father, Gamal Ormson, was treacherously murdered in 1063, and his murderer, Earl Tosti, was deposed and banished for this and other crimes in 1065. Between these two dates, most probably, we must fix the building of this monastery."

The dial at Edston, Yorks, is over the south door, and the shape, the carving, and the lettering of the inscription are exactly like the dial at Kirkdale.

The inscription would seem to be incomplete ; it reads : " ✠ Lothan me wrohte a " (" Lothan wrought me "), and over the dial is carved in letters which are mutilated in the middle: "✠ Orlogi . . . viatorum ✠" ("The time-teller of travellers").

There are other dials of a similar kind at Aldborough, Old Byland, Weaverthorpe, etc., in Yorkshire, at Escombe (Durham), Barnack (Northants), and in various parts of England.

An interesting paper on Weaverthorpe Church and its dial, by Mr. John Bilson, F.S.A., has recently appeared in *Archæologia*, vol. LXXII, from which much of the information recorded here is extracted. The late Mr. Haigh gave A.D. 952 as the earliest date to which this dial could be referred, but this is now shown to be wrong, and the dates of the church and the dial have been proved, by the inscription on the latter, to be within the first decade of the twelfth century.

The dial is situated in the tympanum over the south doorway, and consists of a semicircle, surrounded by a double line, and is divided by lines into twelve parts. Every other line has a cross on it and the broken-off gnomon is still to be seen.

The inscription is above the dial and is incomplete at the beginning, where the stone on which it is incised has been cut away, and stops in the middle of a word at the end, probably because the carver had miscalculated the space at his disposal and had no room to finish it. It reads:

> ✠ In honore sci Andreæ
> Apostoli Herebertus
> Wintonie hoc Monasteri
> um fecit in tempore re . . .

This Herebertus Wintonie (the late twelfth-century chroniclers call him Herbert of Winchester) is a very interesting personage, especially to Hampshire people. He is also styled Herbert the Chamberlain, and was the possessor of about a dozen houses in Winchester and outside the West Gate. Holding an official position in the court of the Norman kings, we find him as one of the officers charged with the superintendence of the Survey of Winchester, the so-called "Winton Domesday," of the reign of Henry I.

Thomas II., Archbishop of York (1108–1114), granted a valuable property, which included Weaverthorpe, to this prominent Winchester royal official, and so began his connection with Yorkshire, which ended by his son becoming Archbishop of the Province and his canonization in 1226 as St. William of York.

Weaverthorpe Church is in the main built in the Norman style, but it retains some pre-Conquest characteristics, including the dial, which, however, divides the day according to the duodecimal system and not into the four tides of the Saxon system.

The dial at Escombe, Durham (already mentioned on pp. 10 and 11), is one of the earliest, perhaps the earliest, in association with a church which has come down to us. It is *in situ* in the wall over the comparatively modern porch and has a serpent carved round its upper part. The semicircle is divided on the octaval system into four equal parts or tides. Professor Baldwin Brown, in a new edition (1925) of his book on Anglo-Saxon Architecture, says he has made a special examination of this dial,[1] and in his opinion it is original and *in situ* and dates from the latter half of the seventh century. The book mentioned above, the full title of which is *The Arts in Early England*, vol. II (second edition, 1925), will be quoted in subsequent pages. It is of much interest, for in it the author has drawn up a scheme for the chronology of pre-Conquest churches which will be of great assistance to all students of this period and the help which the writer has obtained from it he now

[1] The dial is illustrated in vol. V, p. 175, *The Arts in Early England*.

gratefully acknowledges. Professor Baldwin Brown
mentions several Saxon sundials, and he attaches considerable value to them generally as an aid in the dating
of churches, " for being of stone and forming integral
parts of the fabric, they imply a church of this material."

In Hampshire there are three Saxon dials, all in an
excellent state of preservation.

The one at Warnford (see sketch) is now built into the
wall over the south door and under a later porch.   It

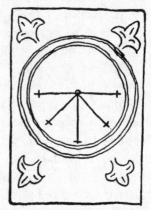

SKETCH OF SAXON DIAL AT WARNFORD.

is carved on a square stone and has a complete double
circle, but the lower half only is divided by three crossed
lines into four equal parts.   Outside the circle the
corners are decorated with a fleur de lys.

Both Warnford and Corhampton (to be described
immediately) are situated in the Meon Valley, the
district occupied by the Jutish settlement of the Meon-
waras, which was evangelized by St. Wilfrid, A.D. 681.

Warnford Church was rebuilt in the twelfth century by
Adam de Port, but it was originally founded by St.
Wilfrid, and these facts are recorded in two inscriptions
still to be seen on the church.

I. Below the dial :

" Fratres orate prece vestra sanctificate
Templi factores seniores ac juniores
Prevavit Wilfrit fundavit bonus Adam modo reno[vavit]."

II. On the north wall :

" Adam hic de Portu solis benedicat abortu Gens cruce signata per quem
sic renovata."

Adam de Port was a great Hampshire landowner and one of the men who signed Magna Carta.

There can be little doubt that this dial belonged to St. Wilfrid's Saxon church, and at the rebuilding of the church in the twelfth century was preserved and transferred to its present position.

CORHAMPTON is a nearly perfect specimen of a Saxon church, possessing pilaster strips, and long-and-short quoins externally, while the chancel arch and north doorway and part of the south doorway show characteristic features of the same style. The Rev. Daniel H. Haigh considered this church and dial to date from St. Wilfrid's time.

The dial (see Plate V) is in its original place in the south wall of the nave, just east of a buttress, which forms part of the south porch, the latter being modern.

It is very similar to the one at Warnford, though larger and more elaborate, and is carved out of a stone somewhat longer from above downwards than from side to side. The workmanship is good, but constant exposure to the elements has, in parts, somewhat worn its surface. The usual two circles (with a projection of quite an inch) are to be seen, the angles of the stone being also filled with a fleur de lys, and in addition between each leaf there is a long, round-ended, projecting ornament. The lower half of the dial was evidently divided by three lines into four equal parts, but the middle line

cannot now be seen as the stone here and also on the
western part of the dial is much worn.   The transverse
line dividing the dial into an upper and lower part is
well shown, except to the west, and a cross is to be
seen at the eastern end of this line and also on the line
below it.   The upper half of the dial has no lines visible,
except a short mark on the west side which may be part
of a line.

Professor Baldwin Brown mentions and illustrates
this dial [1] and compares the foliage on it with the foliage
on a Saxon sundial at Barnack, Northants, and with
that on the carved slabs which fill three window openings
on the tower faces of the same church.   He dates
Corhampton Church as early eleventh century and
Barnack as late tenth century.

The third Saxon dial in Hampshire is to be seen at
St. Michael's Church, Winchester (see drawing), and its

SAXON SUNDIAL, ST. MICHAEL'S CHURCH,
WINCHESTER.

design is exactly similar to that at Warnford and so is
probably of the same date, but the wall in which it is
fixed is several centuries later.[2]   It is carved out of a
square stone, has the same double circle, and the corners
are occupied in the same way by the fleur de lys.

[1] *The Arts in Early England*, vol. II, p. 276 (second edition, 1925).
[2] The church was rebuilt 1822.

The upper part of this dial has no lines and in the lower half the divisions are different on each side of the central perpendicular line. This central line is marked by a cross, and the lower western quarter of the dial is divided into two equal parts by another crossed line. These two parts are each further subdivided by lines into three parts. It will thus be seen that the lower western quarter is divided into six parts, following the duodecimal system of dividing time as seen in our present-day clocks.

The lower eastern quadrant of the dial is divided by three lines into four equal parts, thus following the octaval system ; but whereas the mid-morning line on the west is crossed, it is the line above the mid-afternoon one which is crossed on the east. Haigh thinks this is due to a mistake on the part of the maker of the dial, supposing that he counted three spaces on the east side as he had done on the west and so made the cross unthinkingly.

There are other Saxon dials in various parts of England, but one, of which I have been unable to find any notice in any books to which I have access, is to be seen in the interesting Norman church at Castle Froome, Herefordshire. This dial is situated over the south doorway, but it is very difficult to examine as it is obscured by a later porch, the gable of which almost completely hides it from view. It is carved out of a solid stone and shows only the lower half, which is enclosed in a half-circle of the usual double pattern. This half-circle is divided by three lines into four parts, and on the western side there is another line in addition. This dial, which I believe has so far escaped notice, seems to show the usual characteristics of dials of the Saxon period.

The church of Holy Cross, Daglingworth, Gloucestershire, contains many evidences of its Saxon origin in its long and short quoins, rebuilt chancel arch, small two-light windows splayed on the outside, and four rudely sculptured stones. In addition, there is, over the south doorway and protected by a later porch, a Saxon sundial in an excellent state of preservation (see sketch).

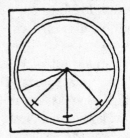

SKETCH OF SAXON DIAL AT
DAGLINGWORTH.

It is carved out of a square stone, with the usual double circle, but is quite devoid of ornamentation. The upper half of the dial is plain, but the lower half is divided by three lines, each marked with a cross, into four equal divisions or tides, and on the western side the upper quadrant is divided into two parts by an additional line which has no cross. This last line marks the position of the Dæg-mæl point, which will be referred to directly. Professor Baldwin Brown considers this church to belong to the early part or middle of the eleventh century.

All these Saxon dials are very much alike in their essential details, being all constructed for the division of time on the octaval system. The day-night is divided into eight tides of three hours each, and the lines seen on their dials marking the *central* point of a tide are generally marked with a cross-line. Occasionally other lines are to be seen dividing the tides into two and in other

instances into three parts, and these secondary lines
are not marked by a cross.

It falls to be observed here that there is one other
mark sometimes to be seen on the face of these dials which
will be found to be of some importance when we are
considering the post-Conquest dials, and special reference
will be made to it in Chapter IX, p. 134 f. (under Steventon). This mark is seen on the dial of Aldborough to be
a form of the swastika or fylfot, but it is marked on the
dial at Kirkdale with a star.[1]

The position on the dials, where this mark appears,
marks the Dæg-mæl point, the beginning of the first
tide of the day, and it corresponds with 7.30 a.m.[2]

The eight tides into which the day-night were divided
are given by Haigh as :

1. Morgan, from $4\frac{1}{2}$ a.m. to $7\frac{1}{2}$ a.m.
2. Dæg-mæl, from $7\frac{1}{2}$ to $10\frac{1}{2}$ a.m. (the first tide of
the day).
3. Mid-dæg, from $10\frac{1}{2}$ a.m. to $1\frac{1}{2}$ p.m.
4. Ofanverthr dagr, from $1\frac{1}{2}$ to $4\frac{1}{2}$ p.m. (the last tide
of the day).
5. Mid-aften, from $4\frac{1}{2}$ to $7\frac{1}{2}$ p.m.
6. Ondverth nott, from $7\frac{1}{2}$ to $10\frac{1}{2}$ p.m.
7. Mid-niht, from $10\frac{1}{2}$ p.m. to $1\frac{1}{2}$ a.m.
8. Ofanverth nott, from $1\frac{1}{2}$ to $4\frac{1}{2}$ a.m.

There can be very little doubt that the Saxon sundial
was used as a time-marker, but if it was constructed
with a horizontal style it must have been so very
inaccurate as to have been almost useless.

In his paper on " Yorkshire Dials," the Rev. D. H.
Haigh gives some information throwing light on the use
of these dials as time-markers.

Ælfric, the grammarian, who lived c. 950–1021, was

---

[1] See Kirkdale dial, p. 14.
[2] It is marked by a line at Daglingworth, p. 22.

an Anglo-Saxon prelate and author, and among his works is a vocabulary which gives us the words " horologium," " gnomon," " dægmǽl " (day-mark), and " dægmǽls pilu " (day-mark's pile), which point out that the dial and the gnomon were the usual instruments for measuring time. And from the same source we find that there was an officer who was called " dægmæl sceawere " or " tidsceawere," i.e. dial or tide-announcer, whose duty, therefore, it was to observe the dial and tell the times of day.

Then in the Glossary appended to Ælfric's Grammar, in the place which dægmæl occupies in the vocabulary above cited, after the words which denote " lamps," " candles," and " snuffers," and before others which denote undoubtedly church furniture, we have " belle," " belle-hús," " litel ,belle," " mycel belle " (one for calling the folks to church and the others for telling the tides).

So the " tide-shower," living about the church, perhaps occupying one of those apartments with which our earliest churches seem to have been always provided, would observe the progress of the shadow and be able to notify the time of day, with sufficient exactness, to all who lived within the sound of the " mickle bell."

That the upper chambers in Saxon church towers and porches were sometimes domiciles of a humble kind for residence is now generally accepted. The occupant was as a rule the ostiarius or sacristan, who kept the doors, safeguarded the relics, and attended to the bells, being bidden in some cases to " ly over nyghtes' therin."

When the Normans conquered England they brought with them the duodecimal system of measuring time which had long been in force on the continent. The day being now divided into twelve hours, the old Anglo-Saxon dials with their four tides to the day became useless. There can, however, be little doubt that a twelve-hour day had been known in England ever since the Roman occupation, and numerous dials now extant point to the fact that the duodecimal and octaval systems were in use side by side at the same time. Probably the Saxonic portion of the population preferred to measure their time by the three-hourly tides, while the descendants of the Romans clung to a day of twelve hours. It is well to bear in mind that the two systems are found combined on the same dial, the addition of a cross on a line being sufficient to mark the pure Saxon portions.

Undoubtedly Norman influence was present in England before the Conquest, but it must have been at about this period that the general use of Mass-clocks was introduced into the land. Probably every church had one, for so far as we know they formed the only means then known in England for the measurement of time. It is true that Alfred the Great had constructed candles, marked off with divisions in such a manner that as the stem burned down so the time could be measured, but these were probably a luxury which only the wealthy could afford. The Mass-clocks were cheap, easily constructed, and very durable, and it seems strange that no written record of them has come down to us. Except for what remains of them, carved on our old church walls, nothing is known, but that they were very numerous seems to be proved by the fact that, notwithstanding the innumerable alterations and additions to which these churches have been subjected and the decay produced by hundreds of years of exposure, yet hundreds of these little time-markers still exist, and carry us back to those early times when the Church was

the centre of the life of the people and not only provided for the spiritual needs of the population, but looked after their material needs, even to supplying them with the correct time.

There is in the British Museum (Tib. c. vi. fol. 7) a drawing of a Saxon dial in a Saxon psalter of the eleventh century ; but so far as I am aware, no drawing or writing having reference to these Mass-clocks has yet been discovered.

A writer,[1] after pointing out how very inaccurate the Saxon sundials must have been on account of their having (as he thinks most likely), a horizontal gnomon, goes on to say that this inefficiency is one reason why such time-tellers are so rare between the twelfth and sixteenth centuries. And yet in Hampshire alone there are scores of these dials still remaining, and this in a county where the most ruthless " restoration " and rebuilding of churches have taken place. As an example of the number of these old time-keepers still extant, the county of Somerset may be taken, in which there are nearly 500 parishes, and Fr. Horne gives a description of 224 dials which he has found there.

To assign an absolute date to a Mass-clock is at present quite impossible. A dial incised on a Norman doorway may quite possibly have been placed there one or two hundred years after the doorway was built, but very occasionally a hint as to the age of a dial may be obtained from some architectural detail with which it is associated.[2] It may be assumed, and it is probably true, that soon after the Conquest[3] these dials came into general use and that they continued in

---

[1] Victoria County History, *Hants.*

[2] See descriptions of dials at Chalton, Idsworth, Bridge Sollars, etc.

[3] Chap. IX, Steventon, p. 136.

use until clocks were invented, or perhaps it would be more correct to say, until clocks became common.

Before concluding this chapter it may be of interest to give some few particulars about clocks, with the dates of some well-known ones, with a brief mention of ring-dials and the large scientifically constructed sundials often to be seen on churches at the present day. Finally, the puzzling question as to how time was measured in the medieval period on sunless days and during the night must receive some comment.

Clocks were first used in England in the thirteenth century. Westminster Abbey had one in 1288 and Canterbury soon afterwards. At Exeter Cathedral some of the wheels of a clock are still in motion and the oldest of these wheels is said to have been working more or less regularly for about 700 years. The clock at Wells Cathedral dates from c. 1390.

These earliest clocks were, as one would expect, only found in the great cathedrals, and when they were provided with a face or dial it was always set up, not outside, as is usual to-day, but within the building. The dial-face, outside the church, in connection with the clock was not introduced till the fourteenth century, and even in the early part of the seventeenth century village church clocks often had no dial-face.

The parish churches doubtless followed the example set by the cathedrals as soon as they could afford the expense, but in country districts we may well suppose that many, many years elapsed before the remote churches had any more reliable time-keeper than the little Mass-clock; indeed, there are many ancient churches now standing which it would seem never have had a clock.

Nevertheless, by the fourteenth century clocks must have become fairly common, especially in towns, for, according to Dr. Cox, in every set of churchwardens' accounts of the fourteenth and fifteenth centuries which are yet extant, mention is made of the repairs to the church clock or the providing of a new one.

A ring-dial, which could be carried in the pocket, and which told the time when held up in the sunlight, was known in Shakespeare's day and is mentioned in *As You Like It.*

The scientific construction of sundials made great progress during the sixteenth and seventeenth centuries, and the large dials constructed on these principles, which are now sometimes seen on churches, generally date from the end of the seventeenth or the beginning of the eighteenth century. A very early one is recorded in the churchwardens' accounts of St. Mary's, Warwick, of 1676 : " Paid for making Sunn dyall £4 " ; and there is still to be seen on South Damerham Church, Hants, a very primitive specimen, dated 1708. On the porch at Ellingham there is a fine large dial, dated 1720, and at Warblington another dated 1781, and of course there are numbers of others all over England.

Sometimes they seem to have been made for a special purpose, for the wardens' accounts, 1597–8, at St. Martin's, Leicester, have an entry which reads : " For 3 yardes of great Wyer to make a Soon Dyall with which Master Belgrave made to set the Clock by at the end of the new Ospitall   xii^{d}."

Over the south porch of Bromsgrove Church, Worcestershire, there was formerly one of these dials inscribed in Old English characters : " We shall dyal " (i.e. " We shall all die "). In Ledbury Church, Herefordshire, a glass sundial has been preserved together with its metal gnomon. It no doubt was once in a window on the south of the church, where it would tell the time both inside and outside, but is now preserved in a window in St. Katharine's Chapel.

The time-markers in England, from the earliest times of which we have any certain knowledge, were then, first, the Roman dials, then the Saxon dials, and then the Mass-clocks or primitive sundials, and lastly clocks and the scientifically made sundials; but the last, which perhaps were preferred on account of their comparative cheapness, became obsolete with the advance of the railway.

It may also be noted that from the very earliest times all these various means of recording the passing hours were connected with the fabric of the church, and at the present day the most usual place in any small town or country village where a clock can be found is on the parish church.

The problem of the measurement of time in the medieval period on sunless days, and before sunrise and after sunset has now to be considered. This difficulty applies especially to the greater churches, but in a lesser degree the same problem is met with in the small country parishes. Time-markers of some kind must, one would imagine, have been a necessity, for a regular succession of services was usual both by day and night.

In the tenth century the so-called Canons of Elfric direct the holding of services at the seven canonical Hours, namely, Prime about 4 a.m., Matins at 6 a.m., Terce at 9 a.m., Sext at noon, Nones at 3 p.m., and Vespers and Nocturns. At a later period the saying of the canonical Hours was restricted to the religious houses and monasteries, and the public services of the parish churches were mostly confined to Matins, Mass and Evensong, in which the canonical Hours were "accumulated" and abbreviated.

In many churches the day-bell was rung *in aurora*

diei, i.e. between dawn and sunrise, and was immediately followed by the " morrow-Mass," an early Eucharist chiefly maintained to enable travellers and those engaged in early-morning duties to attend divine worship.

The hours of the successive services both in the day and in the night varied at different periods, and there were local customs which caused variations, but sufficient has been said to show that there were both in towns and in the country many services during the time when a sun-dial would be useless. For an account of the times of the ordinary round of services in the medieval period the reader may be referred to the chapter on " Daily Life in Church and Close " in Professor Hamilton Thompson's book, *The Cathedral Churches of England*.

In addition to the night services, we have to consider how the time was ascertained on days when there was no sunshine, and in this connection the ordinary parish church is more directly concerned.

It may at once be acknowledged that we do not know for certain how time was regulated in the absence of sunlight. Some method or methods must have been in vogue, for there is no doubt that all the various services went on with unfailing regularity all over the country. There *may* have been clocks, but we have no records of them before the thirteenth century and they must have been very rare for a long time subsequently.

Perhaps the stars were utilized as time-markers on clear nights, and perhaps the sand- or hour-glass was employed ; but when it is remembered how common the water-clock in its various forms was among the Egyptians, Greeks, and Romans, it would be remarkable if some form of this device for measuring time was unknown in England. Of all these things we have no certain knowledge, but bronze bowls, with a tiny hole in the lower part, have been found and it has been suggested that they acted as water-clocks while slowly filling, and the writer would suggest that the cresset-stones which are found in monasteries may have had each of their cups filled with a measured quantity of fat or tallow, the burning of which, by occupying a definite period of time, would enable them to be used as time-markers.

It is just possible that we in this age of clocks, watches, and other artificial aids have lost what may be called the *sense of time*, which our ancestors may have possessed to such an extent as to be of practical use to them. The country-man to-day will often ask, " What is the *right* time ? " and he probably knows the time (? sun-time) to a certain extent, but he wishes to know what time it is by the watch, and everyone must have met certain people who have this sense of time in a most remarkable degree and who can always tell the time with astonishing accuracy.

" Time and tide wait for no man."

CHAPTER III
DESCRIPTION OF MASS-CLOCKS

CONTRARY to what one would perhaps expect, these dials vary in form, size, detail and position in the most remarkable manner. Few indeed can be found which exactly resemble one another in every particular. Their variety is so great that it seems useless to try to classify them according to their shapes and details. They all, however, have this in common—they all have a central hole, the style-hole, in which the gnomon or style was fixed and from which the lines, if there are any, radiate.[1] This general appearance may be gathered from the photographs.

THE STYLE-HOLE

The style-hole is generally of rounded form, and it may be quite small or in proportion to the size of the dial comparatively large. Very often the hole is now blocked up with cement or plaster,[2] but if not, the depth appears to vary considerably. Frequently the hole is in a stone or quoin,[3] but perhaps almost as often it is in the masonry joint between two or more stones,[4] and in the latter case it is now always blocked up by the pointing of the joint. Square style-holes are somewhat rare, but occur at Newton Valance, Warndon (Worcs.), and Downton,[5] near Salisbury.

THE GNOMON OR STYLE

The gnomon fitted into the style-hole and projected

[1] See, however, p. 42: Dials without Style-hole. [2] Cheriton, Plate III; Houghton, Plate VIII. [3] South Hayling No. 1, Plate IX. [4] Chaddesley Nos. 2 and 3, Plates IV and XII; Herriard No. 3, Plate VIII. [5] Plate V.

from the face of the dial, and it was the shadow of this
in the sun's rays that marked the time on the dial face.
No complete, unbroken gnomon has come down to us,
but in a number of cases broken-off pieces have been
observed in the style-hole.   At Brockenhurst the style-
hole retains its gnomon of metal, broken off and projecting about $\frac{1}{16}$th of an inch.   The diameter of the
projecting part is less than $\frac{1}{8}$th of an inch.   At Warblington the remains of the style can be seen in the hole.
It is of soft metal, possibly laten.   At Laverstoke
there is a small piece of style remaining.   This seems
to be of iron, with its red stain on the stone round it.
The remains of styles can be also seen at Chaddesley
Corbett, Newton Valance, etc.   Pieces of wood have
been found in style-holes, and in some cases have been
extracted from them, but it seems exceedingly doubtful if
such a perishable material was often used for the style.

We know nothing as to the length of the projecting
part of the gnomon or of its thickness.   Too long a style
would have the disadvantage of being easily knocked
against, and the opposite, having too short a shadow,
would be inconvenient, and it is to be remembered that
the length of the shadow on a dial varies with the
position of the sun, and the orientation of the dial also
influences it.

As to the diameter of the style, a very thin one would
show no shadow at all on a somewhat dull day, and
with one too thick the shadow would be so wide as to
be confusing on these small dials.

From the construction of some dials [1] it would almost
seem probable that one side of the shadow was the part
intended to act as the time-teller, but generally the
central part was used.

Dials are occasionally found which have two parallel

[1] Chilcomb, Plate VI.

vertical lines to mark noon,[1] and in such cases it is reasonable to suppose that midday was marked when the shadow fell between these lines.

It has been generally assumed that the gnomon projected from the style-hole horizontally, i.e. at right angles to the plane of the dial, but this is purely a supposition and is not based on any known facts. Against this theory is the fact that if it did project in this manner, then the dials were almost useless as time-tellers ; but we will leave the consideration of the direction of the gnomon to a later chapter.

The idea that a movable object, such, for instance, as the church key, could be used as a style, is almost too absurd to merit consideration, because the slightest variation in the inclination of the key, either to the east or the west or upwards or downwards, might, and generally would, cause a considerable error in the time registered. A believer in this idea should visit some dial and, trying to forget, as far as he is able, the time of day, he should determine that he will find out when, for instance, it is 9 a.m. or noon ; he has only to make a few experiments and he will soon be convinced how impossible it is to be even fairly accurate.

The question of movable styles will be referred to again towards the end of this chapter.

LINES

The majority of Mass-clocks have, radiating from the style-hole, a number of lines. In many cases these lines radiate in all directions, upwards and downwards and to the right and left. These have generally been known as *wheel dials*, and the term is a convenient one and may be applied not only to those which have twenty-four

---

[1] Sherborne St. John No. 2, Plate VI.

well-marked lines,[1] but to those many others where
some of the lines have been obliterated by the weathering
of the stone or have been mutilated in other ways,[2]
and also to those dials which seem always to have been
composed of a few less lines, one or two being missing
here and there, but for the most part seem to conform
with this type.[3]

The lines at their circumference frequently are contained in a circular line, but this does not seem to be an
important part of the dial and is often omitted altogether
or in part.   It seems to be a relic of the Saxon dials.

Half-wheel dials, formed of the lower half only of a full-
wheel dial, are of frequent occurrence,[4] but one formed
of the upper half only is, if not unknown, very rarely
found ; such a dial, *in situ*, has never been described.[5]

Quarter-wheel dials are seen on some churches and
these seem to be more frequent when there are a number
of dials on the same building.   Perhaps they are of
comparatively late date, for many of them appear to be
sharply cut and not much weathered.   The quarter-
wheel may be either the western or left-hand [6] or the
eastern or right-hand quadrant, but always in the lower
half of a circle. Dials showing the eastern quadrant seem
of much less frequent occurrence than those showing
the western ;   they are, in fact, exceedingly rare.[7]

It must not be supposed that in these half- and
quarter-wheel dials all the lines are present, for frequently some are absent, and especially so in the case
of the upper lines.

In addition to the above, there are many dials which

[1] Barfreston No. 7, Plate I ; King's Somborne No. 1, Plate IX.
[2] Martin No. 1, Plate X.
[3] Sherborne St. John No. 2, Plate VI.
[4] Bishop's Sutton No. 3, Plate IX ;   Chaddesley No. 3, Plate XII.
[5] Baughurst No. 1.   A reversed dial.   Plate XII.
[6] Herriard No. 4, Plate VIII ; Stoke Charity No. 3, Plate XIII ;
Barfreston Nos. 3, 4, 6 and 8, Plate I.   [7] Himbleton, sketch, p. 197.

vary in the most irregular manner, both as to the number of lines and the angles at which they are cut.

Sometimes the vertical or horizontal lines or both are not incised on the stone, but advantage is taken of joints in the masonry, and the junction between two or more stones takes the place of an incised line. This method of saving trouble in the making of a dial is frequently met with.[1] At Up Nateley the chamfered edge of a window-sill forms the horizontal lines.

Occasionally the lines of a dial extend over two or even over several stones (without using the masonry joints), as in the dial over the south doorway at Sherborne St. John's Church, where the lines are incised over five voussoirs, and the dial at Downton occupies parts of three stones. Plate V.

In length the lines vary, not only in the various dials, but also in the same dial, and sometimes they are much longer on one side than on the other, as for instance in the one just referred to at Sherborne St. John's Church, where the length varies from $7\frac{1}{2}$ to 18 inches. Lines having a length of about 4 inches are perhaps the most common, but lines of 10 inches or more are not unknown, and occasionally a dial, such as the one at Compton in Surrey, is met with with lines only about $1\frac{1}{2}$ inches long.

The cross line, so characteristic of the Saxon sundial, is very rarely seen on Mass-clocks, but for examples of this peculiarity the reader is referred to the illustrations of the dials at Sherborne St. John No. 3, Plate XV, and Baughurst No. 2, Plate II.

The lines on dials differ in the way they are made, and that not only on different dials but also on the same dial. Some are clear, straight incisions such as might be made

---

[1] Chaddesley Corbett No. 2, Plate IV, and No. 3, Plate XII,; Bishop's Sutton No. 3, Plate IX ; Barfreston No. 3, Plate I.

by a chisel, others might possibly have been scratched
on the stone with a nail.

One line deserves particular notice, the so-called
Mass-line. It is sometimes to be observed in the lower
left-hand quadrant, as looked at, and is often better
marked than the other lines, being perhaps straighter,
more sharply cut and often deeper.[1] This line has been
assumed by Fr. Horne to be the Mass-line, the line
which marked the time when Mass was said, and he
considers it generally corresponds with the position of the
figure VIII on a watch, and that it marks 9 a.m., which
was the usual hour for Mass on Sundays and holidays.

There is much to be said in favour of this theory, and
it will be discussed in some detail in a subsequent chapter.

It may be well to point out here that the lines on a
Mass-clock generally mark the *commencement* of the hours,
whereas on a Saxon dial the ordinary lines, which are
usually crossed, mark the *middle* of the tides. (See p. 22.)

HOLES

These form a very conspicuous feature of many dials,
but they are not by any means always present.

The most common situation in which they are found
is at the end of a line, and in some dials every line is seen
to end in a hole. In such an example, instead of a line
forming a circle at the circumference, its place may be
taken by the ring of holes, as at Martley, Plate X.

A hole at the end of a line seems often to have been
used to emphasize its importance, and perhaps for this
reason one may often be seen at the end of the noon-line,
as at Herriard No. 3, Plate VIII. Holes may entirely
take the place of lines, as in the very clear example at
Herriard No. 1, Plate VII, or there may be a circle of
holes with short lines extending only part of the way to

---

[1] Warnford Nos. 1 and 2, Plate XIV.

the centre, as at Breamore No. 2, Plate II, and Martley, Plate X.

Dials composed solely of holes are exceedingly difficult to discover on some walls, and this is especially the case in Hampshire, where so many of the ancient churches are built of Binstead stone, which is covered with innumerable holes. This characteristic of Binstead stone is well seen in the photograph of the dial at Chilcomb, Plate VI.

Some of the holes, viz. those of good size and of some depth, were perhaps made to contain pegs and so were more easily seen ; they may also have been used sometimes in the construction of the dial, to form a fixed point to place a ruler against when making a line. Many of the holes, on the other hand, are not much more than dots and can never have held a peg.

Sometimes these small holes are so disposed that a number of concentric circles or parts of circles are formed, as is well seen in the dial at Stoulton, Plate XI, and it may be possible that in such dials an attempt has been made to measure the length of the shadow.

REVERSED DIALS

Numerous dials in a reversed position, that is, having lines radiating upwards from the style-hole, have been noticed in various parts of England,[1] and there seems to be an unusually large number of these in Hampshire. The churches in this county have been very unfortunate in that so many of them have suffered, particularly during the last century, from a perfect orgy of restoration, and this may account for so many reversed dials here.

So far as can be ascertained, there has nowhere been found a dial in a reversed condition which is absolutely certainly in its original position. It is a remarkable

[1] Baughurst No. 1, Plate XII.

fact that great care seems to have been taken, whenever a stone with a dial on it was moved, to turn it upside-down. A stone forming part of the moulded jamb of a doorway seems not only to have been reversed, but on account of its moulded angle to have been also removed from one side of the doorway to the opposite side.[1] Why this was done we can only conjecture.

The question arises, Was a dial in a reversed position of any use as a time-teller ?

The upper half of a wheel dial, which is in fact an upside-down dial, is different. These dials are in most cases *in situ* and it would be extremely interesting to know why a dial of this sort was made. Perhaps it was copied from the Saxon dial, and there is no doubt it is more symmetrical and, to the ordinary observer, looks more as a dial should look.

But there are other considerations. A dial such as this fitted with a style pointing due south *and with the style bent upwards* will have a shadow at noon exactly on the upper vertical line. From experiments with dials of this variety I have no doubt the time could be told with a fair degree of accuracy for the other hours of the day by using styles bent to different angles, but it seems to be a much more complicated matter than with the lower half of a dial. There seems to be no reason why the style should not be divided on leaving the style-hole, one part remaining horizontal or being bent down-wards, while the other part might be bent upwards.

On the other hand, there seems to be no reason to mark noon or any of the other hours in the upper half of the dial, for this could be done equally well in the lower half.

The question must await further investigation, and

[1] Winchfield Nos. 1 and 2. Notice the letter A, in the lower left-hand corner. Plate XV.

it may be that the shadow in the upper half was used to correct inaccuracies in the lower half.

WHERE TO LOOK FOR MASS-CLOCKS

Generally dials will be found on the south side of the church, but those which have been moved from their original positions may be found facing east, west or north. Occasionally they are even found inside the church.

Their position on the south wall varies considerably and is influenced to some extent by the material of which the walls are chiefly composed. It is useless, for instance, to look for a dial on a wall composed entirely of flints.

Apart from this, perhaps the most common place is the south doorway, on the right- or left-hand jambs of which or on both they are frequently to be seen, and yet when one is pointed out to regular church-goers, they will almost always tell you that they had never noticed it before.

The jambs or arch of the priest's doorway in the chancel are also common positions, and a south buttress or the sill or side of a window. The quoins at the south-east or south-west angles of the church are also very favourite places, and, as Fr. Horne has pointed out, if you approach the church by the usual path, whichever of these portions you come to first, there it is usual to find the dial.

It is not at all unusual to find a dial or dials on a porch, it may be of fifteenth-century date, and, on the jambs of the Norman or Early-English south doorway covered by it one or more other dials rendered useless by the later building. In this and in other ways a dial may be of assistance in dating a portion of a church, for if a transept, vestry or buttress, etc., causes a dial to be in the shade, it may be surmised that the projecting part is of more recent date than the wall on which the dial is incised.

As to the height at which dials are placed, this is generally about the height of an observer's eyes, but it varies considerably. At Preston Candover there is a dial, probably *in situ*, on a level with the ground, but the earth has probably been thrown up on this side of the church.

On the other hand, some dials are so high as to be almost out of sight, such, for instance, as the one at Himbleton, which is 15 or 20 feet from the ground, and the dials at Headbourne Worthy and Sherborne St. John are about 9 or 10 feet from the ground.

Whatever may have been the case in the past, it would seem that now the larger churches, the cathedrals, abbeys and minsters do not possess Mass-clocks. It is on the walls of our village churches that they are most often to be observed, but small town churches sometimes possess one, and occasionally one may be found on the walls of a city church.[1]

COPY DIALS AND EXPERIMENTAL DIALS

The name " copy dials " has been given to dials, badly and clumsily made, which are often found by the side of, underneath, or near another dial or dials. Sometimes there are several of these roughly scratched dials on the same church wall, and Fr. Horne suggests that they are possibly the work of " an idle boy with a knife." This is a quite possible explanation for some of them, but may not many of them be what may be called " experimental dials " ?

These dials were almost certainly made by a local man, possibly by the village priest, and not by a skilled hand who went round the country making them for the

[1] St. Martin's, Salisbury. Since the above was written dials have been found on St. Michael's and Holy Rood, Southampton.

various churches. That being so, it seems probable, seeing how much they vary, that an experimental dial would first be scratched, and when it had been tested by observation, a more deeply cut and perhaps a more accurate one would be made, taking the first as a pattern.

Examples of such imperfect, experimental dials with the more perfect dial below may be seen in the photos taken at Idsworth, Plate IX, and Burghclere Nos. 6 and 7, Plate III.

MULTIPLE DIALS

Many churches possess several dials, and it seems probable that some of these were for special purposes, such as the marking of a certain church service,[1] or certain particular hours,[2] but probably in most instances they were fitted with a permanently fixed style and served to tell the time at different seasons of the year, a special dial for each season. This subject will be more fully considered when dealing with the " Bent-Style Theory " in Chapter V.

DIALS WITH NO STYLE-HOLE

Very rarely a dial is found which seems to have no style-hole and in which it is impossible to suppose one ever existed. There are, of course, many dials which have the style-hole blocked up with cement, and in some cases this has been applied in such a manner as to suggest at first sight that no hole ever was present. A careful examination will generally, however, prove that a hole formerly existed. Apart from these, there are dials which appear to have the usual characteristics of position, size, lines, circle, etc., but in which no trace of a central hole can be found.

Of course if these are really dials, a style must have been provided, and if two pieces of wood or metal are

[1] Burghclere No. 5, Plate II.   [2] Herriard No. 1, Plate VII.

jointed together at the ends in much the same manner as
a modern carpenter's rule, it might be possible to make
a style by placing one piece in contact with the wall,
perhaps between marked points, and then bending the
other piece to a right angle or any other angle. I am
indebted to Mr. W. J. Andrew, F.S.A., for this suggestion
and it certainly seems to offer a solution of a difficulty
which is otherwise inexplicable.

Perhaps pieces of metal, not hinged, but bent to
certain angles, were used, and if these were placed
between marked points on the dial very efficient styles
would be obtained.

Styles of this kind, provided with a stud at the back,
may have been used for those dials, of which there are a
large number, the style-holes of which are very shallow.
The projection at the back would be placed in the
shallow depression, and this would help to fix the position of the style while it was held against the wall by the
hand. One might even suggest that a style constructed
on this principle and having two studs, one at each
end, might prove quite satisfactory for dials such as
Herriard No. 3, Plate VIII, or Burghclere No. 5, Plate II,
where the upper stud would be fixed in the style-hole and
the lower one in the hole which can be seen vertically
below it.

ORDNANCY SURVEY BENCH MARKS OR "BROAD ARROWS"

These marks are often to be seen on church walls, and
it may be well to issue a warning against mistaking them
for Mass-clocks. The Victoria County History, *Hants*,
in the description given of the church at Bishop's
Sutton, Hants, says there are two dials on the south-
east corner of the nave. A photo of this corner showing
presumably the marks referred to is to be seen on

Plate IX. The lower of these is undoubtedly an Ord-nance Survey bench mark, and with regard to it and to these marks in general the Director-General of Ordnance Survey, Colonel E. M. Jack, has very kindly furnished me with the following particulars :

" The sizes of these marks vary considerably in England and Wales, but the symbol is always the same, i.e. the broad arrow, commonly known in country districts as the crow's foot. There is always a horizontal bar cut, the gnomon being a copper bar or bolt, approxi-mately 6 inches in length, inserted in the stone, with a horizontal bar cut on it and fixed with lead run around it. This is always described as a bolt. The horizontal bar is used by the leveller, who inserts the angle-iron on it to enable him to obtain the necessary readings; the heights given on the Ordnance Survey Maps showing a are always taken at the horizontal bar."

" These marks were first cut during the early part of the last century," and this particular one, at Bishop's Sutton, was " cut on July 3, 1863."

These marks, then, are not dials, but are cuts on stones to enable calculations to be made to ascertain the height of the place above the sea-level. The broken-off bar of copper in the centre and the lines radiating from it may cause a superficial observer to mistake them for Mass-clocks. It is an interesting fact that the " broad arrow " as a Government mark was first used in the reign of Queen Elizabeth. She appointed Sir Henry Sidney to be Master of the Ordnance, and he, finding that the Government effects were constantly being stolen, caused everything under his charge to be marked with his own heraldic badge, the pheon. Since that time the " broad arrow " has been retained as the official Govern-ment mark.

CHAPTER IV

EXPERIMENTAL DIALS

It has been assumed hitherto in these pages that the marks we have been considering were cut on church walls for the purpose of recording time, but in order to prove this (if indeed proof is necessary, for hardly anyone nowadays doubts it) and for the much more important object of endeavouring to ascertain how that purpose was fulfilled, the writer made and set up a number of Experimental Dials.

The object in view was to observe and record the position of the shadows cast by the sun on dials having various aspects and fitted with styles set at different angles. The results of these observations, which extended over the whole of a year, are contained in this book, and as experiments such as these have, so far as can be ascertained, never been made before, it is hoped that many doubtful points will be made clear. It will also be proved quite definitely that the dials were capable of being used as time-tellers and that they could perform that duty with a quite sufficient degree of accuracy.

The dials employed were made of pieces of white cardboard, about 5 inches square, and after the lines had been accurately drawn and numbered, a style-hole was made in the centre, and they were fixed on a dial-board with drawing-pins.

The lower half of a dial only need be described, the upper half being an exact counterpart. The half-circle, having a horizontal line at the top, was divided by eleven lines, 15 degrees apart, just as a compass is divided. (See diagram of the Standard Dial.) The horizontal line on the left was marked 0°, the next 15°, and so on to the perpendicular line 90°, and in the same manner up the right-hand side, ending with the horizontal line 180°.

The part between each two lines is therefore equal to 15 degrees, and this was divided again by shorter lines into three equal parts of 5 degrees each. It will be apparent by reference to the diagram of the Standard Dial that the lines numbered 0° to 90° stand for the hours VI a.m. to XII, and the lines 105° to 180° for the hours I to VI p.m. As there are 15 degrees between each line it is obvious that 1 degree is equal to 4 minutes. The shadow moving round a dial such as this is capable of marking the time from 6 o'clock in the morning on the left-hand side to 6 o'clock in the evening on the right-hand side. But most of the dials experimented with proved to be, as was expected, far from accurate ; but by recording the position of the shadow as covering such and such a degree from hour to hour and from day to day, the exact amount of the inaccuracy was ascertained.

The method of marking by degrees was adopted to obviate the confusion which would have been caused by marking by hours and minutes, for suppose at 9 a.m. the shadow fell on the line 15, it is much better to register this as 15 than to say that at 9 o'clock the shadow fell on 7 o'clock.

The styles used in these experiments were made from old bicycle spokes, and most of them were fixed at right angles to the plane of the dials, but some were bent at various angles, as will be explained when describing each dial individually.

For the complete understanding of these experiments it is necessary to describe the wooden structure on which the cardboard dials were fixed (see photo, Plate XVI).

A piece of wood 3 feet broad, 2 feet high and 1 inch thick was procured, and the material chosen was teak, as this was said to be least likely to warp. Two strong square posts were then taken and set firmly in cement in holes in the ground and in such a manner that the board when fixed to them would face due south.

It is by no means an easy task to get the board fixed exactly right. A plumb-line is the best instrument to show the right position in the vertical direction, and a compass is essential to ascertain that the board faces due south. In using the latter, the error (variation) of about 12° to 14° west must be allowed for. The needle of the compass does not point to the true north and south, but about 13° west of north and 13° east of south. The true position for the board therefore is facing 13° east of south by the compass.

In order to make experiments with dials facing not due south but which are turned more or less to the east or to the west, an addition was made to the structure.

A board was fixed along the bottom of and at right angles to the original teak board. This formed a shelf which was firmly fixed and made horizontal by means of a spirit-level.

Six boards were then cut, in such a manner that each could stand up firmly on the shelf while its bevelled edge fitted accurately against the teak board at the back. These six boards were arranged along the shelf in the following manner. The first at the east end was made to face 15° east of south, the next 30° east of south and the third 45° east of south. The three boards at the west end were made to face 15°, 30° and 45° west of south.

The six boards were not made fixtures, but stood up in grooves cut in the shelf, because it was necessary to move them at certain times, i.e. early morning and late afternoon, when one board might be in the shadow caused by the board or boards between it and the sun. Each of the boards had a dial fixed on its face.

There only remained to provide suitable protection against the weather. This was found in a sloping roof with boarded front and sides, fitting closely and hinged to the shelf below, in such a manner that the whole could be easily opened from above and turned on the hinges downwards.

In small dials such as these experimental ones, and the same applies to the real Mass-clocks, it is impossible to be strictly accurate so far as minutes are concerned. The position of the shadow when it falls between the sub-divisions has to be guessed, and it is also to be remembered that the shadow is considerably wider than a line. Also, in the country, Greenwich time was difficult to ascertain and the Greenwich time as supplied by the local Post Office cannot always be relied upon. Another factor which makes accuracy difficult is the absence of strong sunlight. The sun may be strong enough to cast a shadow near to the gnomon, but not strong enough for the shadow to be very distinct at the circumference of the dial.

One or other of these difficulties may cause slight errors in the position of the shadow, as shown in the records, in individual cases, but taken as a whole, the records are believed to be substantially correct.

The records were taken for a whole year, but are of necessity somewhat irregular, as of course they can only be obtained when the sun shines. For the purpose of comparison they were taken only at fixed times, and the fixed times chosen were the hours.

It must be plainly understood that a sundial does not pretend to register Greenwich (Clock) Time : it simply registers the time as shown by the sun, which is called " Sundial Time " or " Apparent Solar Time."

Clock Time and Sundial Time are sometimes, but very rarely, the same, but on most days in the year they differ, and the difference between the two is called the " Equation of Time."

Clocks and watches are adjusted to tell Mean Solar Time, or Greenwich Mean Time, or, as it is usually called, Greenwich Time. The Mean Solar Day is constant in length, but what is called the " Apparent Solar Day " varies because the movement of the earth in its orbit round the sun is not constant on account of the ellipticity of the orbit, and also because the axis about which the earth rotates is not perpendicular to the plane of its orbit. Sundials do not register Greenwich Time, but what is called "Apparent Solar Time," and this is affected by the two causes mentioned above, which make the length of the Solar Day not uniform.

Sundial Time (A.S.T.) at Greenwich differs from Greenwich Mean Time (Clock Time) by the " Equation of Time," and the former can be obtained from the latter by adding or subtracting the " Equation of Time." This differs by a certain number of minutes each day, and the number of minutes to be added or subtracted can be found in most almanacs.

Another adjustment had to be made to correct the difference in longitude between Greenwich and the place (near Romsey, Hants) where the dials were set up. This place is about 1½ degrees west of Greenwich, and as for every degree 4 minutes have to be allowed, 6 minutes had to be added on to Sundial Time at Greenwich.

These two adjustments are best explained by taking an example. Suppose a record is to be taken on May 1 at 9 Sundial Time. At what time by the watch shall the record be taken at Romsey? Sundial Time at Greenwich is 9 h. and on May 1 the Equation of Time is 3 m.; therefore Greenwich Mean Time is 8 h. 57 m. But it will be 6 minutes later before the same phenomenon occurs at Romsey, and therefore the correct time to make the record is 9 h. 3 m. by the watch.

Another method of arriving at the same result is: You want to find the time by the watch (G.M.T.) when Sundial Time (A.S.T.) is 9 a.m. on May 1. A.S.T. 9 h. — Equation of Time 3 m. = Local Mean Time 8 h. 57 m. The longitude of Romsey is $1\frac{1}{2}$ degrees, or 6 minutes, west, and therefore the Greenwich Mean Time is 6 minutes greater.

$$8 \text{ h. } 57 \text{ m.} + 6 \text{ m.} = 9 \text{ h. } 3 \text{ m.}$$

The time, adjusted in this way, was always used in making the records, but for the sake of simplicity it is omitted from the printed tables.

Having ascertained the correct time to observe the shadow and make the record, Dial I is now inspected and the shadow is seen falling on 44. The record is then written: May 1, Dial I, $\dfrac{9{\cdot}3}{44}$, and on reference to the Standard Dial it is seen that the dial on this date and at this time is registering practically the correct time, being, at most, 4 minutes slow.

A table is given on the opposite page showing the correct times for making the records at this place (Romsey) for each day in the year, but no notice has been taken of odd seconds, and the nearest minute is given for each day.

TABLE SHOWING THE CORRECT TIMES TO MAKE RECORDS AT 1½° W. OF GREENWICH, TAKING INTO ACCOUNT LONGITUDE AND EQUATION OF TIME

Add to Greenwich Time or Subtract:

	mins.		mins.		mins.
Jan. 1	add 9	Apr. 28 to 30	add 3	Sept. 29, 30	sub. 4
2, 3	,, 10	May 1 ,, 6	,, 3	Oct. 1	,, 4
4, 5	,, 11	7 ,, 22	,, 2	2 to 4	,, 5
6 to 8	,, 12	23 ,, 31	,, 3	5 ,, 8	,, 6
9, 10	,, 13	June 1 ,, 6	,, 4	8 ,, 12	,, 7
11 to 13	,, 14	7 ,, 11	,, 5	13 ,, 16	,, 8
14, 15	,, 15	12 ,, 16	,, 6	17 ,, 22	,, 9
16 to 18	,, 16	17 ,, 20	,, 7	23 ,, 31	,, 10
19 to 22	,, 17	21 ,, 25	,, 8	Nov. 1 ,, 14	,, 10
23 ,, 26	,, 18	26 ,, 30	,, 9	15 ,, 19	,, 9
27 ,, 31	,, 19	July 1 ,, 5	,, 10	20 ,, 23	,, 8
Feb. 1 ,, 24	,, 20	6 ,, 12	,, 11	24 ,, 26	,, 7
25 ,, 29	,, 19	13 ,, 31	,, 12	27 ,, 29	,, 6
Mar. 1	,, 19	Aug. 1 ,, 8	,, 12	30	,, 5
2 ,, 5	,, 18	9 ,, 14	,, 11	Dec. 1, 2	,, 5
6 ,, 9	,, 17	15 ,, 19	,, 10	3, 4	,, 4
10 ,, 13	,, 16	20 ,, 23	,, 9	5, 6	,, 3
14 ,, 17	,, 15	24 ,, 26	,, 8	7 to 9	,, 2
18 ,, 20	,, 14	27 ,, 30	,, 7	10, 11	,, 1
21 ,, 23	,, 13	31	,, 6	12, 13	,, 0
24 ,, 26	,, 12	Sept. 1, 2	,, 6	14, 15	add 1
27 ,, 30	,, 11	3 to 5	,, 5	16, 17	,, 2
31	,, 10	6 ,, 8	,, 4	18, 19	,, 3
Apr. 1 ,, 2	,, 10	9 ,, 11	,, 3	20, 21	,, 4
3 ,, 6	,, 9	12 ,, 14	,, 2	22	,, 5
7 ,, 9	,, 8	15 ,, 17	,, 1	23 to 25	,, 6
10 ,, 13	,, 7	18, 19	,, 0	26, 27	,, 7
14 ,, 17	,, 6	20 to 22	sub. 1	28, 29	,, 8
18 ,, 22	,, 5	23 ,, 25	,, 2	30, 31	,, 9
23 ,, 27	,, 4	26 ,, 28	,, 3		

Having, over the space of twelve months, made careful records of the position of the shadow on fifteen Experimental Dials, it now became necessary to compare these records with the photographs of actual dials as found on church walls, and to ascertain, so far as possible, how the latter were used for the purpose of telling the time.

For the purpose of comparison a fixed standard is required, and this was found in a circle divided into 360 degrees, a copy, in fact, of an experimental dial with the addition of Roman numerals to mark the hours. A representation of such a dial—the Standard Dial—is to be found on p. xx.

A standard to work to having been obtained, the next thing is to examine photographs of actual dials. A tracing of a photograph is made, and for this purpose the tracing paper used by architects is very useful.

The next proceeding is to enlarge the dial, and this is done by prolonging each line, and the enlarged copy is now examined with a little instrument called a "protractor."

A protractor is in shape a hemi-circle, and is made of a thin transparent material. On it are marked a centre and radiating lines and the circumference is divided very accurately into 180 degrees, the degrees being numbered at intervals. It is in fact exactly similar to our Standard Dial, but has no clock-hour numbers. With this little instrument it is possible to compare the copy of an actual dial with the Standard Dial. The tracing of the dial is laid on a flat surface and the protractor placed on the top of it, the centre marked on the protractor being placed over the centre of the style-hole. The tracing can be seen through the transparent protractor, and the prolonged lines extend beyond its edge, and so, taking the protractor as a guide, each line can be marked with the number of the degree to which it exactly corresponds.

To make the use of the protractor clear it may be well to take an example. A photograph of the dial at Up Nateley will be found on Plate XIV, and an enlarged tracing with each line numbered on p. 139. These numbers show the exact angle, measured in degrees,

which each line forms, and they can be compared with
those on the Standard Dial.

Hours		VI	VII	VIII	IX	X	XI	XII	I	II	III
Up Nateley	.		20°	32°	49°	60°	77°	90°	105°	124°	136°
Standard	.	0°	15°	30°	45°	60°	75°	90°	105°	120°	135°

This demonstrates that the dial at Up Nateley and
the Standard Dial, however different they appear on
mere inspection, are in reality extremely alike, and
shows with a great amount of certainty that the maker
of the Up Nateley dial intended to place the lines 15
degrees apart.

The position of the lines on a dial may also be compared with the records of any experimental dial, and
if at any period of the year the two coincide, the inference
can be drawn that the dial was made to tell the time for
that period.

The dial at Up Nateley faces S. 32° E., and although
it is not now *in situ*, it probably originally had a very
similar aspect, and one of the Experimental Dials, Dial
VI, faces S. 30° E. The two are therefore very much
alike, and the records of Dial VI in the month of June
show that the angles very nearly correspond with those
cut on the Up Nateley dial. To make this plain, the
numbers are set out thus :

Hours		VI	VII	VIII	IX	X	XI	XII	I	II	III
Dial VI	.	18°	28°	42°	58°	75°	90°	103°		125°	nil
Up Nateley	.	20°	32°	49°	60°	77°	90°	105°	124°	136°	

The angles are here seen to be somewhat alike, and
the dial at Up Nateley may *possibly* have been used, with
a straight style set at right angles to its plane, to tell
the summer time, but it would only remain fairly accurate for a short time, and in the afternoon it would be
very inaccurate.

This example is only given to show one of the ways in which the records may be utilized.

As to the Up Nateley dial, it will be shown later that, fitted with suitable styles, it is capable of marking the time all the year round.[1]

It is now necessary to give a few words of explanation about the records. I have in front of me the figures marking the position of the shadow of the gnomon on fifteen dials on most days throughout a year, and they cover fifty-nine large sheets of paper. To a few readers —shall we call them experts ?—these figures might prove interesting, but those of my friends who are best qualified to give advice on this subject tell me that the best plan will be to publish only a few of these records, and even in the cases where a record is given to cut it down to the smallest amount possible.

It is very doubtful if many readers would take the trouble to wade through the mass of figures of which the records are composed, and I shall therefore endeavour to state as clearly as possible the conclusions which can be arrived at and the deductions which can be drawn from the experiments, premising only that these conclusions and deductions are founded on the figures which are in my possession which cover the whole of the hours of the day from 6 a.m. to 6 p.m. Occasionally it will be necessary to quote figures in detail from the records for the sake of the argument, but generally the tables given will only show the position of the shadow at the middle of each month, and this only for the hours 9 a.m., noon, and 3 p.m.

Having seen how the Experimental Dials were made and the method employed in recording the position of the shadow, we may now examine the records of two dials, viz. Dial I and Dial XII.

[1] See Analysis, Chapter IX, p. 139.

DIAL I

Aspect, due south. Gnomon at Right Angles to Plane

Hours in Greenwich Time .	IX	XII	III
January . . .	13°	90°	165°
February . . .	21°	90°	159°
March	33°	90°	149°
April	40°	90°	139°
May	45°	90°	134°
June	48°	90°	131°
July	47°	90°	133°
August	42°	90°	140°
September . . .	36°	90°	145°
October	26°	90°	155°
November . . .	16°	90°	165°
December . . .	11°	90°	166°

The figures show the position of the shadow at the middle of each month.

DIAL XII

Aspect, due south. Gnomon points due south, and is turned down to form an Angle of 62° with the Vertical

Hours in Greenwich Time .	IX	XII	III
January . . .	38°	90°	138°
February . . .	42°	90°	138°
March	46°	90°	134°
April	49°	90°	131°
May	51°	90°	129°
June	53°	90°	127°
July	52°	90°	129°
August	49°	90°	132°
September . . .	47°	90°	133°
October	43°	90°	137°
November . . .	41°	90°	140°
December . . .	38°	90°	137°

Dial I faces the south exactly, and its style, which is a straight one, is fixed at right angles to the plane of the dial, i.e. it projects horizontally and also points due south. This is the position for the style which most people consider to have been the one always adopted by the makers of these dials.

The numbers (which show the position of the shadow)

should be examined in the abbreviated records here given and compared with the numbers on the Standard Dial. If this is done, a fair idea will be obtained of the accuracy or otherwise of this dial as a time-marker; if the numbers correspond, it is marking the time accurately, and vice versa.

The most striking thing to be noticed in the records of this dial is that throughout the whole year, day by day and week by week, the shadow caused by the sun at noon is always on the vertical line marked 90°. In other words, this dial always tells the exact time at noon. It is advisable to grasp this fact, for this is the only dial, with a gnomon at right angles to its plane, which marks noon correctly throughout the year.

As will be shown later, every dial but this one which faces due south—viz. those which face either east of south or west of south and have a style fixed at right angles to their planes—fail to mark noon correctly.

That is the first and most important fact to be observed in the records of Dial I, viz. noon is correctly marked always. The next thing to observe is that the figures correspond with a fair degree of accuracy from about the middle of April to about the middle of August.

Note the figures 47° and 133° in July, this month being the one when the time is most nearly accurate. They should be 45° and 135°, and so the difference is only 2 degrees, an error of only about 8 minutes. The figures are not given for the hours X and XI or I and II, but they are of course still more accurate. On the other hand, the early hours and the late ones are not quite so correct. It will thus be seen that Dial I keeps practically correct time for four or five months in the year.

On the other hand, the records disclose a very different state of affairs in the winter. The figures at the end of December, the time when they are most inaccurate, are

10° and 166°, whereas they should be 45° and 135°, so that the dial now, at 9 o'clock, has a shadow marking 6.40 a.m., and at 3 o'clock it is marking a few minutes past 5 p.m.

From a consideration of these facts we may conclude that a dial similar to Dial I would be quite a good time-keeper round about midsummer, but would be quite useless during the winter months.

Now observe, and this is most important, how the same dial acts if it is furnished with a *bent* gnomon. Turn to the records of Dial XII, which has exactly the same orientation as Dial I, but has a bent instead of a straight gnomon, and compare the records of the two dials with the Standard Dial.

Here are the figures for the end of December:

Hours			IX	X	XI	XII	I	II	III
Standard	.	.	45°	60°	75°	90°	105°	120°	135°
Dial I	.	.	10°	24°	47°	90°	*	156°	166°
Dial XII	.	.	37°	54°	73°	90°	107°	125°	135°

* No records were taken at 1 o'clock.

These figures show that although the shadow was caused to fall at angles which were not quite correct, yet the bent gnomon has produced a very considerable improvement, and turned an absolutely useless dial into a fair time-keeper, and there can be no doubt that by a suitable adjustment of the gnomon strict accuracy could have been obtained.

Again, compare the records (which are here given) of the two dials at the spring (*a*) and autumn (*b*) equinoxes:

Hours		VIII	IX	X	XI	XII	I	II	III	IV
Standard	.	30°	45°	60°	75°	90°	105°	120°	135°	150°
Dial I $\begin{cases} a \\ b \end{cases}$			34°	48°	67°	90°	*	130°	147°	160°
			33°	48°	67°	90°		132°	148°	160°
Dial XII $\begin{cases} a \\ b \end{cases}$			47°	62°	77°	90°	*	118°	131°	148°
		32°	46°	61°	75°	90°		119°	135°	149°

* No records were taken at 1 o'clock.

Here Dial I is always about three-quarters of an hour wrong, while the bent style has caused Dial XII to register approximately the correct time. The records of these two dials prove conclusively that a Mass-clock can be used as a real and correct time-marker if the gnomon be suitably adjusted. With the result of these experiments in front of one, a dial could now be made which would be still more accurate ; but with nothing to guide one, the style had to be fixed at an angle which it was hoped would give good results. It will be observed that only one alteration of the style has been required, during the year, to obtain these results ; but if stricter accuracy is advisable, it could easily be obtained by using four styles instead of two.

Two separate, but similar, dials were used in this experiment, each fitted with a different style, but exactly the same result could have been obtained by the use of one dial and changing the style.

CHAPTER V

THE BENT-STYLE THEORY

In making the experiments recorded in these pages, the writer's purpose was not so much to construct a dial or dials which would accurately mark the time, as to ascertain the principles upon which dials could be constructed to fulfil that purpose. As the experiments proceeded, it became obvious that alterations of the gnomon, i.e. alterations of the angle which it formed with the vertical face of the dial, and in many cases alterations ·in the direction towards which it pointed, would tend to keep the shadow on the correct lines, and so would enable the time to be told with accuracy.

Further observation showed that a dial might be quite accurate for certain hours in the morning but very inaccurate for hours later in the day, and vice versa. From these facts it might be thought that, in order to obtain the correct time, two styles would have to be employed, the one early in the day, and the other later, but that is not so.

The following extracts, taken from the records of Dials V and XIII in April, prove this, and the "Standard" is added to show what the numbers ought to be :

Hours . . .	IX	X	XI	XII	I	II	III	IV
Dial V . .	47°	66°	86°	104°	*	135°	145°	154°
Dial XIII . .	50°	63°	76°	90°		122°	137°	150°
Standard . .	45°	60°	75°	90°		120°	135°	150°

* No records were taken at 1 o'clock.

Dial V is here seen to be recording the time at 9 and 10 o'clock with a fair degree of accuracy, but from 11 to 4 o'clock the times are very far from correct.

Dial XIII, on the other hand, records the whole of the hours very accurately.

Now, both these dials face S. 15° E., but Dial V has a straight gnomon fixed at right angles to its plane, i.e. also facing S. 15° E., whereas Dial XIII has a bent style which points due south and forms an angle of 70° with the vertical face of the dial.

This and other similar facts having been ascertained, viz. that the correct time could be obtained by alterations of the gnomon, a great point was gained. The difficulty was to know when to change the gnomon. Now the experiments are concluded, and with the records as a guide, it is possible to say the gnomon should have been changed on such and such a date on this dial or on that, but with no data available such a proceeding was impossible. The writer was content to change the style as seldom as possible, and generally only when the dial had become very inaccurate. A mathematician could no doubt work out the best angles for the gnomon and the best times for changing it, but so far no one with the necessary knowledge has undertaken this work, and it is to be presumed the makers of these dials had to proceed by observation and experiment.

With the help of the records now obtained, there is no doubt a better result could be arrived at by experiments carried on for another year, and so on for several years before the strictest accuracy obtainable was attained. But that is not the writer's object: all that he has aimed at is the principle, and not the details, and this object there is every reason to believe has been attained.

This principle is embodied in what may be termed the

"Bent-Style Theory," which will be described at the end of this chapter.

It has generally been assumed, but, so far as the writer knows, upon no evidence whatever, that the gnomon projected horizontally from the dial. In the Victoria County History, *Hants*, Vol. III, p. 240, the following statement is made : " No Saxon sundials now existing have preserved the gnomon, but it is most likely that it projected horizontally."

Dom Ethelbert Horne, in his book *Primitive Sun Dials or Scratch Dials*, says (p. 18) : " The gnomon or style that cast the shadow was a peg that stood out at right angles from the face of the inscribed stone."

The late Rev. Daniel Henry Haigh in his classical paper on Yorkshire dials says (p. 136) : " The presumption is that the gnomon was always perpendicular to the plane of the dial."

It has been generally recognized that a horizontal gnomon will not register the correct time, but no one seems to have pointed out how very incorrect the time would be if registered in this manner.

To show this inaccuracy, some figures have been extracted from the records of seven dials, each fitted with a horizontal, straight style, for the month of January, at 9 in the morning.

Month of January.			*Time, 9 o'clock.*				
Dial	I aspect due S.		Average time shown by dial 6.50 a.m.				
,,	II	,,	S. 45° W.	,,	,,	,,	,,	Nil.*
,,	III	,,	S. 30° W.	,,	,,	,,	,,	6.45 a.m.
,,	IV	,,	S. 15° W.	,,	,,	,,	,,	6.40 a.m.
,,	V	,,	S. 15° E.	,,	,,	,,	,,	7.20 a.m.
,,	VI	,,	S. 30° E.	,,	,,	,,	,,	8.10 a.m.
,,	VII	,,	S. 45° E.	,,	,,	,,	,,	12 to 2 p.m.

* During January there is generally no shadow on this dial.

Inaccuracies such as the above can be found in the

records over and over again, but only one more instance need be given. Suppose you wish to have your lunch at 12 o'clock and you decide to be guided as to the time by the Dials II to VII, then you may vary the time of the feast from about 7.30 a.m. to 8.15 or 9.20 a.m., or 2.30 p.m. or 3.45 or 4.30 p.m., according to which dial you happen to look at.

Dials II and VII are of course exceptional dials, but the others are not, and many dials can be found on church walls with similar aspects. Dials which register the time four hours wrong would certainly be useless, and we may be quite sure that some method of measuring time more accurately than this was in vogue before clocks were invented.

It may be granted that strict accuracy was unattainable with these dials, and that the difference of fifteen minutes or even half an hour would not greatly matter in medieval times when there was no fixed standard of time, and when such a standard was not required; but a time-marker which was apt to be from two to four hours wrong would, even in those times, be useless.

At this point it will be convenient to make a few further observations about the style-hole and also to consider the material or materials which were used in the construction of the gnomon. The noon-line will then be dealt with, and then we will try to imagine how an unskilled person could make a Mass-clock.

If a careful examination is made of a number of dials, one of the characteristics which first strikes an observer is the large size, in many examples, of the style-hole, and its rounded and worn appearance. This is amply accounted for if the gnomon was constantly being removed and replaced; but if the gnomon was a fixture, it is difficult to see how it was caused. No doubt at first the hole was small, only sufficiently large to admit a small metal rod. When by constant friction it became so large as to allow movement to take place, the shadow would be apt to be cast on the wrong place and accuracy of time would be lost. In such a case the easiest remedy would be to procure a thicker style. This in time would also wear away the stone and become loose and inaccurate. As there is an obvious disadvantage in having a very massive, thick style, the remedy would be to plug the hole with wood and bore a hole for the style into the latter. That this was done there is every reason to believe, for from the style-holes of several dials pieces of wood have been extracted, and it is probably these pieces of wood that have caused various observers to entertain the idea that the original gnomon was of wood and therefore must have projected horizontally from the face of the dial. The more reasonable explanation is that the wood was only used to plug a hole which friction had caused to be too large, and into this wood a metal style was inserted in much the same way as picture-hangers plug the wall nowadays before driving in a large nail.

In the case of a dial facing exactly south it has been pointed out, when Dial I was examined, that for a part of the year a straight style was required. For such a dial a wooden style would be suitable, and there is no reason why a style of this material should not have been used except that wood is more perishable than metal. For all other dials a bent style is required, and so the material used must have been either iron or latten or some other metal capable of being bent.

By the kind permission of Fr. Horne I am enabled to illustrate here two pieces of styles extracted from style-holes and lent to me for this purpose.

No. 1 at the top is a not quite straight piece of metal, probably iron, which measures $\frac{15}{16}$ths of an inch long and a ¼ of an inch in diameter. The blunt thick end came from the bottom of the hole and the opposite almost pointed end has been produced by exposure.

No. 2 is a slightly tapering piece of wood, 1 inch long and a ¼ of an inch in diameter. The thinner end shows the original slanting cut made to sharpen this part and the thicker end shows an irregular broken surface.

In the great majority of the dials still to be observed on the walls of our ancient churches there is one line

No. 1.

No. 2.

BROKEN PIECES OF STYLES EXTRACTED FROM STYLE-HOLES.

which is almost constantly present, viz. the line which descends from the style-hole perpendicularly downwards. There can be little doubt that this line was meant to mark noon, and if the wall faced due south and the gnomon also projected due south, the shadow at noon would undoubtedly fall on this line. An examination of the south walls of churches soon discloses the fact that in many instances the orientation is inexact ; they sometimes face due south, but very often there is a deviation of several points either to the east of south or to the west of south, and in many cases the deviation is considerable. In these numerous instances where the dial does not face the south exactly, if it were fitted with a style at right angles to its plane, the shadow at noon would not fall on the vertical line.

The following figures taken from the records of various dials in the early part of February will make this point clear. The records in each case were made at noon, and the times registered by the dials vary from 8 a.m. to 4 p.m.

Dial I.   Faces due south.   90° = 12 o'clock.

Dial	II aspect S. 45° W.	Shadow on	32° =	8 a.m.
„ III	„ S. 30° W.	„	43° =	9 a.m.
„ IV	„ S. 15° W.	„	58° =	10 a.m.
„ V	„ S. 15° E.	„	122° =	2 p.m.
„ VI	„ S. 30° E.	„	137° =	3 p.m.
„ VII	„ S. 45° E.	„	150° =	4 p.m.*

* The reader is advised to refer to the Standard Dial.

It will thus be seen that the only dial (No. I) which gives noon correctly is the one on a wall facing exactly south, and this is just the position which is not often found.

It is now purposed to describe how a man devoid of any knowledge of scientific dialling might be supposed to have made a Mass-clock, and in doing this we shall ascertain how the inaccuracies just mentioned were overcome.

The dial maker, I imagine, found a convenient stone on the south wall of his church, and having made a hole, he fixed into it a straight metal style, and then cut a line extending from it perpendicularly downwards. This was to be his noon-line. He did not worry about the orientation of the wall, that did not matter one iota to him ; but at noon he bent his style,[1] at the point nearest to the wall, to such an angle as would cause the shadow to fall exactly on the perpendicular line. He would, as a matter of fact, bend the style into a position pointing due south, but would not require to have the knowledge as to which was the exact south, and probably he was without that knowledge.

It may be asked how did the man know when it was

---

[1] Laterally, i.e. either to the east or to the west.

exactly noon, and it may be answered that noon is the time when the shadow caused by the sun falling on a pole stuck upright in the ground is shortest. This fact was known from very early times, and the Greeks are known to have ascertained the time by measuring the length of a shadow : they talk of a six-foot shadow and a ten-foot shadow.

A dial made in the manner described above, with a style deflected so that it pointed due south, would mark noon all the year round.

The importance of this cannot be over-estimated. By the bending of the style, when necessary, to the right hand or to the left, the shadow was always caused to fall on the vertical line at noon, and this on every dial in spite of all differences due to orientation. And not only this, but the shadow continued to fall on the vertical line on every day throughout the whole year, in fact for ever, so long as the gnomon and dial lasted. An absolutely mathematically correct fixed point had been found, and one which had this further advantage, that it divided the day into two parts, which, generally speaking, were fairly equal.

This seems, in all probability, to have been the first step in the making of a dial, and the next would be to mark out further divisions to show the various hours.

It is to be remembered that the maker of a dial at this period was not without patterns in his own country, for the Anglo-Saxons had dials of very excellent workman-ship, a considerable number of which remain to this day. But the Anglo-Saxons measured time on the octaval system and divided the day-night into eight equal divisions.

After the Norman Conquest, the Roman or duo-decimal system was re-introduced into England, and the day was divided into twelve equal divisions or hours.[1] So our dial-maker in drawing his other lines would follow to a certain extent the Anglo-Saxon pattern with which he was familiar, but he would divide the day into twelve equal parts.

He would observe that on a Saxon dial there is a horizontal line drawn through the style-hole from side to side and serving to mark the division between day and night, and he may have copied this. In addition to this, experiment and observation would teach him that a horizontal style at the equinoxes, when the day and night are equal in length, has a shadow which is horizontal at 6 a.m. and 6 p.m., and so he would cut his horizontal line in accordance with this fact to mark those hours.

The completion of the dial would now be a simple matter, in that all that would be necessary would be the division of the spaces between the 6 a.m. line and the noon-line, and the 6 p.m. line and the noon-line, each into six equal parts. In this manner the lower half of a circle could be made with equal divisions marking the hours from 6 in the morning to 6 in the evening, and if a complete circle was required (a so-called wheel-dial), this could be easily made by cutting above the horizontal line an exact copy of the part below that line. A simple method of doing this would be to extend, to the required distance, each of the eleven lines below the horizontal one.

A dial similar to the " Standard Dial " would thus be procured, and most of the dials now to be seen on church walls are either similar to this or modifications made on this pattern. There are many half-wheel dials and quarter-wheel dials and a vast number of

[1] There can be little doubt that before the Conquest some dials, made on the duodecimal system, were to be found in England (see pp. 8 and 25).

others, the lines or holes on which are constructed
on the same principle, viz. the spaces between them
measure 15 degrees or multiples of 15 degrees, although
some of the lines may be missing.

Having made his dial-face, it may be supposed our
dial-maker next proceeded to experiment with the style,
and in the course of these experiments we may readily
understand that he soon found the horizontal variety
of styles gave, at certain periods of the year, very
disappointing results. He was thus led to use a style
bent down at an angle and so obtain more correct time.

Sometimes, no doubt, he would try to attain his
object by altering the position of the lines on the dial-
face, but experience would teach him that it was far
easier to alter the angle of his style.

In consequence of the great variation in the orientation
of the south walls of churches, every parish would have
to face a different problem, and no doubt many dials
were made which were only experimental and of little
use ; but there can be little doubt that eventually
dials of the wheel variety, with lines 15° apart, were
eventually evolved.

The bent-style theory is now brought forward to
show that approximately correct time can be registered
on the great majority of Mass-clocks by using, when
necessary, a bent gnomon instead of the straight one,
which has generally been supposed to have been the
only kind employed.

To obtain the correct time with a dial facing due
south, the style only requires bending (when necessary)
in one direction, i.e. downwards. With all other dials
the style has to be bent in two directions : it must be
bent laterally to face due south, and it must also be bent
downwards.

The facts, that the straight style cannot give the

correct time and that the bent style can be made to do so, are, it is believed, amply proved by the records of the experiments here brought forward.

In favour of the theory the following considerations may be mentioned. A dial constructed on these principles is quite easy to make, and requires no special skill or expert knowledge. The priest or sexton could easily construct one. Such a dial has the immense advantage of always marking noon correctly, and thus an absolutely fixed point in the twenty-four hours is obtained, and by suitable alterations of the gnomon the approximately correct time can always be obtained.

It is quite in accordance with this theory that dials should have been used in several different ways. One dial only may have been incised on the church wall and from time to time various styles having different angles could have been fitted into its style-hole. Or several dials may have been cut, each fitted with its appropriate style and intended to mark the time at various seasons of the year—a dial for each season. Or a special dial may have been made to mark a particular time, viz. the time of Mass, and such a dial with several styles bent at different angles could have been made to give the time very accurately. Or, again, it might have been necessary to know the time very accurately for two or three particular hours, and in such a case a dial such as the one at Herriard [1] with holes for 10, 11 and 12 would have been very useful, and, if it was furnished with two or more bent styles, the time would have been registered very correctly.

The theory fits in quite well with the idea that on many dials there is one well-marked, distinctly-cut line marking the time for the service of Mass, and generally called the Mass-line. It does not matter at what angle

[1] Plate VII, No. 1

this line is incised (it will be pointed out on p. 88 that these lines are at various angles) ; a series of styles can be made such as would always cause the shadow to fall on this line, and so the correct time for the service would be arrived at approximately.

If the " bent-style theory " be accepted, it follows that these dials were real time-tellers or time-markers, and did more than mark the times of church services, but their usefulness for the latter purpose would thereby be increased. The church clock at the present day not only gives the time for the service, but it also tells the bell-ringer when to ring the bell, and the people when to prepare to start for church, and there is no reason why these ancient dials could not have fulfilled the same purposes.

CHAPTER VI

SOME MORE EXPERIMENTAL DIALS

In Chapter IV a dial was examined which faced due south, and it was there shown that by changing the gnomon once a correct time-marker could be obtained which would be available for use throughout the year.

The same result, as will now be demonstrated, can be obtained on dials which do not face exactly south, but deviate to some extent either to the east or to the west.

In order that this may be made plain to the reader, some figures extracted from the records of two more of the writer's Experimental Dials will here be given.

These dials, Nos. IV and XV, both faced 15 degrees west of south, but whereas Dial IV was furnished during the whole year with a straight style projecting horizontally at right angles to its plane, Dial XV had three styles, all of which pointed due south,[1] but differed in that they were bent downwards to form the angles 23°, 45° and 64° with the vertical. When one of these became inaccurate, it was changed for the second; and when this also ceased to mark the correct time, the third was substituted, but only three changes were made throughout the year.

It must be understood that these dials were only experimental, and it is not claimed that the angles to which the styles were bent were the best possible angles which could have been employed, nor that the times in

---

[1] And so were *not* at right angles to the plain of the dial.

the year when they were changed might not have been altered with advantage. Very probably, styles having somewhat different angles and changed at different seasons would have given better results.

Two figures are given for each dial, and they show in degrees the highest and the lowest during the year under each hour. By comparing these figures with the Standard Dial, the position of the shadow on the dials will be easily seen.

Hours	IX	X	XI	XII	I	II	III
Correct angles (Standard Dial)	45°	60°	75°	90°	105°	120°	135°
Dial IV	{ 7°	15°	27°	43°	*	141°	162°
	{ 48°	58°	70°	83°		113°	129°
Dial XV	{ 30°	47°	68°	90°	*	109°	119°
	{ 51°	65°	78°			125°	141°

* No records were taken at 1 o'clock.

The three styles were used thus :

Angle 23° from the middle of March   to middle of November.
  „   45°   „   „   November   „   February.
  „   64°   „   „   February   „   March.

It is during the winter months that the greatest difficulty is experienced in adapting the gnomon so that the shadow keeps on the right lines. During the summer much better results can be easily obtained, for I find, on examining the full records of Dial XV from April to September, that for all the hours from 9 to 2 there was never an error of more than six degrees (twenty-four minutes) during the whole period.

After an examination of the above figures there can be no doubt that Dial XV tells the time more correctly than Dial IV, and it may also be pointed out that whereas the records of the latter cannot be improved, on the other hand, Dial XV, if fitted with more suitable styles and the changes made at better times, could be made to mark the time with still greater accuracy.

A dial facing due south and one facing S. 15° W. have now been examined, not perhaps in great detail, for that would be too tedious, but sufficiently to show what bent styles are capable of accomplishing. Other examples might be given of dials with different orientations, but it would only be labouring the point.

It is believed that the two examples here cited prove that bent styles can be employed on any dial, whatever its aspect, and that sufficient success has been attained to prove that an approximately accurate dial can be thus obtained.

One more Experimental Dial may be examined in this place, viz. Dial No. X. It faces due south, and has a permanent gnomon which also points due south, but it is bent downwards to form an angle of 39° with the vertical face of the dial.

The idea of this dial was suggested to me by a mathematician (my brother, Commander J. G. Green, R.N.), and such a dial, although never quite accurate, gives the best results, all the year round, that can possibly be obtained from any dial without alterations. The records of the dial show that the position of the shadows at the various hours is very regular.

Some figures from the records are here given [1] :

Noon of course is always correctly marked at 90°.

8 a.m. is always about			41°
9 a.m.	,,	,,	57°
10 a.m.	,,	,,	71°
11 a.m.	,,	,,	81°
2 p.m.	,,	,,	111°
3 p.m.	,,	,,	123°
4 p.m.	,,	,,	138°
5 p.m.	,,	,,	159°

[1] Compare with the Standard Dial.

The style on this dial, it should be noted, is fixed at an angle of 39°, and the reason for this particular angle is that this is the angle which is equal to the angle 51° with

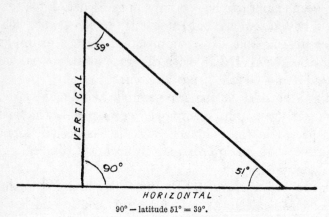

90° — latitude 51° = 39°.

DIAGRAM SHOWING WHY THE STYLE WAS FIXED AT AN ANGLE OF 39°

the horizontal, and 51° is the latitude of Romsey, the place where the dial is set up.   The diagram here given shows this plainly.

From the records given above, p. 73, it is possible to construct a dial-face with the hour-lines drawn at angles

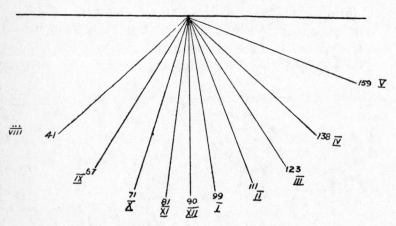

DIAL CONSTRUCTED FROM THE RECORDS OF DIAL X.

which correspond with the position of the shadow as found in the records. A dial-face made in this way is shown here; it was constructed from the records of Dial X.

A dial such as this, provided it faced south and had a gnomon also pointing south and fixed at an angle of 39°, would be a very accurate time-teller throughout the year.[1] This most interesting fact will be again referred to in the chapter dealing with " Various Theories."

[1] This only applies to dials in latitude 51°.

CHAPTER VII

SUNRISE AND SUNSET

IF it be granted that the lines on a half-wheel dial stand for the hours from 6 a.m. to 6 p.m., it then becomes necessary to ascertain if these lines are always useful, or if, under certain conditions, their serviceability is interfered with. In this chapter therefore we will consider the usefulness or otherwise of the various lines as determined by :

    1. The time of sunrise and sunset.
    2. The orientation of the dial.
    3. The declination of the sun.

The time when the sun rises and sets can be found printed in various almanacs, but this is Greenwich Mean Time (G.M.T.), and it is the same all over the country. It has been pointed out in Chapter IV that in considering the time marked by these dials, Sundial Time, or, as it is called, Apparent Solar Time (A.S.T.) has to be used, for of course when they were in vogue Greenwich Time was unknown, and attention has been called to the fact that Sundial Time (A.S.T.) at Greenwich differs from Clock Time (G.M.T.) by the " Equation of Time."

Bearing these considerations in mind, let us take the 6 a.m. line and see how its usefulness is affected by sunrise and sunset. It is obvious that there cannot be any shadow on a dial, however oriented, before the sun rises nor any shadow after the sun has set.

Suppose we take a dial at Greenwich, facing due south, and see how sunrise and sunset affect the usefulness of the 6 a.m. line. In the early part of the year the sun has not risen at 6 o'clock, and the first day when it rises at 6 is March 19. On this date sunrise at Greenwich is at 6 h. 8 m. (G.M.T.), and to obtain Sundial Time the equation of time (8 minutes) must be subtracted thus $6.8 - 8 = 6$ Apparent Solar Time (A.S.T.). The 6 a.m. line on a dial at Greenwich facing due south therefore begins to be of use on March 19.

How long does this line remain serviceable? On what date does the sun cease to rise before 6 o'clock? On September 25 the sun rises at Greenwich at 5.52 (G.M.T.) + equation of time $8 = 6$ (A.S.T.). Therefore the 6 a.m. line ceases to be serviceable after September 25. In a similar manner the usefulness of the 6 p.m. line can be worked out, and also the usefulness of the lines 7 a.m. and 8 a.m. and the lines 5 p.m. and 4 p.m.

The following table shows how the time of sunrise and sunset affects the serviceability of various lines on a dial facing due south, in the latitude of Greenwich.

The 6 a.m. Line.
Serviceable from March 19 to September 25.

The 6 p.m. Line.
From March 18 to September 23.

The 7 a.m. Line.
Serviceable from February 17 to October 25.

The 5 p.m. Line.
From February 17 to October 26.

The 8 a.m. Line.
Serviceable from January 8 to December 6.

The 4 p.m. Line.
From January 8 to December 5.

Throughout the year the sun always rises before 9 a.m. and sets after 3 p.m., so that, so far as sunrise and sunset are concerned, the lines 9 a.m. and 3 p.m. are always serviceable.

The above table applies to Greenwich and to all

places in the same latitude, for a sundial fixed at any place in the world in the same latitude would show the same sundial time (A.S.T.) at any given time and date. Romsey is in about the same latitude as Greenwich, and the longitude is $1\frac{1}{2}°$ W., which is equal to 6 minutes. Sundials placed at Greenwich and Romsey will on May 1 each mark the time of sunrise at 4.38 (A.S.T.); but if you wish to calculate it in terms of Greenwich Mean Time (i.e. by your watch), it will be 4.35 at Greenwich and 4.41 at Romsey.

The effect of sunrise and sunset on the serviceability of the various lines on Mass-clocks may be simply stated thus :

The 7 lines from 9 a.m. to 3 p.m. are useful throughout the year.
 ,,   9 ,,   ,, 8 ,, 4   ,,   ,,   for about 11 months.
 ,, 11 ,,   ,, 7 ,, 5   ,,   ,,   ,,   ,, 8 ,,
 ,, 13 ,,   ,, 6 ,, 6   ,,   ,,   ,,   ,, 6 ,,

The lines on either side, in the upper part of a dial, being the least serviceable, it might be expected that they would often be omitted, and such in fact is the case.

Many dials can be found which only show lines or holes in the lower, central part, and several are illustrated, viz. Timsbury,[1] Himbleton,[2] Barfreston Nos. 5, 6 and 8,[3] Laverstoke,[4] Herriard Nos. 1, 4 and 5,[5] Penton Mewsey,[6] Sherborne St. John No. 1,[7] Burghclere Nos. 1 and 2,[8] etc.

The orientation of a dial determines to a great extent which of the lines on it are serviceable and which are useless.

A dial facing to the *east* of south will make use of the lines 8, 7 and 6 a.m. to a greater extent than a dial facing due south, and, contrariwise, the lines 6, 5 and 4 p.m. will be less serviceable than on a dial facing due south.

On the other hand, a dial facing somewhat to the *west*

---

[1] Plate XIV. [2] P. 197. [3] Plate I. [4] Plate X.
[5] Plates VII and VIII. [6] Plate XI. [7] Plate VI. [8] Plate III.

of south will mark the evening hours to a greater extent than a dial facing due south, but the lines marking the morning hours will be less serviceable.

To take extreme examples, on June 21 on my Experimental Dial VII, which faces S. 45° E., there is a shadow at 6 a.m., 7 a.m., etc., but no shadow at 2 p.m., 3 p.m., etc. ; whereas on Dial II, which faces S. 45° W., there is no shadow before 11 a.m., but a shadow is recorded at 7 p.m.

Thus on Dial VII the lines 6 a.m. to noon are serviceable and the lines 2 p.m. to 6 p.m. useless ; and on Dial II the lines 6 a.m. to 10 a.m. are useless and the lines 11 a.m. to 6 p.m. are serviceable.

On the other Experimental Dials the differences due to orientation, though not quite so marked, are still quite apparent.

In the morning the sun casts a shadow earlier on a dial facing east of south than on a dial facing due south, and still earlier than on one facing west of south.

It might therefore be expected that dials on churches facing east of south would have lines extending higher on the left-hand side, i.e. in the upper part of the left quadrant. This expectation is not realized by an examination of a large number of actual dials ; but it is possible that when the early hours of the morning were required to be marked, a wheel dial or half-wheel dial was made.

The sun in the afternoon casts a shadow later on a dial facing west of south than on a dial facing due south, and still later than on one facing east of south.

Therefore one might expect to find on those dials facing west of south that the lines extended higher up on the right of the vertical line, i.e. in the upper part of the right quadrant. But this also is not the case, as shown by an examination of the actual dials.

The fact is, there are very few dials with lines in the right quadrant only, and the evidence of Mass-clocks goes to prove that the time in the morning and early afternoon was of more importance to the makers than the later hours of the day, although there are, of course, a very large number of complete wheel dials and half-wheel dials, and these probably marked the time from sunrise to sunset.

The declination of the sun is the angular distance between the sun and the celestial equator.

At the equinoxes the sun rises due east on the equator, and the declination is 0°.

At midsummer the sun rises north of east by an amount which differs with the latitude. Thus in latitude 51° N. at midsummer, when the sun's declination is 23½° N., the sun rises bearing about N. 51° E. and sets bearing N. 51° W.

At midsummer, therefore, the sun rises 39° north of east (90 − 51 = 39) in lat. 51° N.

Similarly, in midwinter the sun rises 39° south of east at places in lat. 51° N.

If the records of the shadows on the various Experimental Dials be carefully examined, some of the results there noted are, to anyone unacquainted with astronomical phenomena, both confusing and inexplicable. Take; for instance, Experimental Dial No. III, which faces S. 30° W. At 9 a.m. there are records of shadows on this dial in January, February, March and April, but in May, June, July and August there are records stating that *no* shadow is present. In September, October, November and December the shadow is present again.

Now, the " man in the street " would probably come to the conclusion that if the sun cast a shadow on a dial at a certain hour in the winter, it would most certainly do the same during the summer months.

But in this conclusion he would be wrong, and the reason for this seeming contradiction is to be found in what is called the " declination of the sun."

As a result of this declination, the sun rises to the north of east, i.e. behind the dial, during the summer months, and that being so, there can be no shadow on this dial in the early morning, nor will there be a shadow until the sun rising less and less to the north eventually rises in due east and to the south of east, and this does not happen in the case of this dial facing S. 30° W. until the latter part of August. From this date onwards there will be a shadow on this dial at 9 a.m. right through the winter months down to the latter part of April, when, in consequence of its declination, the sun again rises too much to the north of east for a shadow to be formed.

The declination of the sun therefore influences the usefulness of some of the lines on a Mass-clock, as in the instance given above, where it causes the 9 a.m. line on the dial to be useless during a period extending from towards the end of April to towards the end of August.

The same thing happens on all dials, however oriented. Take one more example. Dial I faces due south, and the records show that at midsummer no shadow is present on the dial at 6 or 7 a.m., notwithstanding that at this period of the year the sun rises before 4 o'clock. But at midsummer the sun rises 39° to the north of east, and it is not until the equinox in September that a shadow is possible on this dial, for at that time the sun rises due east and so begins to shine across the face of the dial. From that time onwards through the winter months, always supposing that the sun rises early enough, there will be a shadow at 6 and 7 o'clock, and this will continue till the spring equinox in March.

It will thus be seen that even on a dial facing due

south there are some lines rendered useless at certain periods of the year by the declination of the sun.

It may also be noted that the declination of the sun causes certain lines in the evening, that is, on the opposite side of the dial, to become useless at certain periods of the year. Thus on Experimental Dial VI, which faces S. 30° E., there are records of *no* shadow at 3 p.m. during the summer, but at the corresponding time in the winter there are records of a shadow being present.

From the foregoing it will be apparent that (1) the time of sunrise and sunset, (2) the orientation of the dial, and (3) the declination of the sun, all have an influence in rendering the upper lines on each side of a half-wheel dial more or less useless at certain periods of the year.

The table given here shows the hours of the day when the relative positions of the sun and of dials set at different angles are such that a shadow may be expected to fall on the dial.

TABLE SHOWING THE TIMES WHEN A SHADOW MAY BE EXPECTED TO FALL ON DIALS SET AT DIFFERENT ANGLES.

S = there is always a shadow. Ss = sometimes, at some period of the year.
N = there is never a shadow.

Hours	A.M. VI	VII	VIII	IX	X	XI	XII	P.M. I	II	III	IV	V	VI
Dial VII S. 45° E.	Ss	Ss	S	S	S	S	S	*	Ss	N	N	N	N
Dial VI S. 30° E.	Ss	Ss	S	S	S	S	S		S	Ss	N	N	N
Dial V S. 15° E.	N	Ss	S	S	S	S	S		S	S	Ss	N	N
Dial I due S.	N	N	S	S	S	S	S		S	S	S	Ss	N
Dial IV S. 15° W.	N	N	Ss	S	S	S	S		S	S	S	S	Ss
Dial III S. 30° W.	N	N	N	Ss	S	S	S		S	S	S	S	S
Dial II S. 45° W.	N	N	N	N	Ss	S	S		S	S	S	S	S

* No records were taken at 1 o'clock.

NOTE.—In order to attain the strictest accuracy the altitude of a dial should also be taken into account; for, to take an example, sunrise would be marked earlier on a dial situated at the summit of a mountain than on one set up in a valley. In the writer's opinion the inaccuracies caused in this way are negligible in the case of the dials described in this book.

CHAPTER VIII

VARIOUS THEORIES

It may be interesting to examine some of the theories which have been advanced from time to time to explain the manner in which these dials were used, the reasons for which they were made, and the objects the makers of them had in view. In doing this, it is not the writer's wish to belittle the work which has been done by others—far otherwise ; but a careful investigation of facts can do no harm, and it is hoped that the records of the position of the shadow, which the writer has collected, at different hours and under various conditions, may throw some light on the difficult problem.

Down to the present time only the fringe of the subject has been touched upon, and it would seem that any further advance in our knowledge must be made by the aid of experiments. What is now needed, when a dial is being examined, is a knowledge of the exact position of the shadow of the gnomon, taking into account the orientation of the dial, the season of the year, the hour of the day and the position of the style, etc., etc., in the place of a vague statement that such and such a line marks the time of a church service or noon, for when an examination of a theory is made upon these lines some quite surprising results can be obtained.

Two theories have been brought forward to explain the objects of these dials, one by Dom Ethelbert Horne, the other by Mr. Rosenberg. These, and perhaps one other, are the only theories known to the writer, but there may be others with which he is not acquainted.

Fr. Horne is the pioneer on this subject, and practically the whole of our knowledge has been obtained from his work. He has told me that he spent eight years collecting information on the dials of Somersetshire, and any opinion expressed by him on the subject must carry great weight.

He does not very definitely set out a theory, but from statements in various parts of his book [1] it is possible to form an idea as to his views.

On p. 3 he writes : " The style is always inserted at a right angle," and " A scratch dial has often only one or two lines, and these, strictly speaking, do not designate *time.*"

On p. 27 : " The scratch dial is in reality a section of a formal sundial adapted for a special purpose, and hence it is not a time-teller but a Mass-marker."

On p. 31 : " Their primitive object undoubtedly was to mark the hour for Mass."

On p. 32 : " A line corresponding with the position of the figure VIII on a clock-face will be 9 a.m. In most churches in pre-Reformation days this was the usual hour for Mass on Sundays and holidays."

On p. 19 he writes that a variation of twenty minutes or so in the time of church services between the summer and winter times would be of little consequence, and it would probably be even an advantage if the services were nearly half an hour later in midwinter than they were in June.

From these extracts it would seem that Fr. Horne's theory may be thus stated :

1. The principal object was to mark the hour of Mass, which was usually at 9 a.m.

[1] *Primitive Sun Dials or Scratch Dials.*

2. That the Mass-line usually formed an angle of about 30 degrees.

3. That a scratch dial is not a time-teller, and that the lines on it do not, strictly speaking, designate time.

4. That the time had arrived for the service of Mass when the shadow on the dial fell on the Mass-line. (This may be inferred.)

5. That the style always projected horizontally, i.e. at right angles to the plane of the dial.

This, then, seems to be Fr. Horne's theory.

Now, a theory stands if it accords with known facts, and it falls if it fails to agree with known facts.

It is proposed to examine the photographs of dials in Fr. Horne's book which show well-marked Mass-lines, and to compare these with the records which the writer has obtained from his various Experimental Dials and ascertain how far this theory agrees or disagrees with the facts which have been obtained from these experiments.

Take, first, the dial at Kilmersdon, illustrated on p. 12 in his book. This, he says, has two lines only, one at about 9 a.m. and the noon-line, and there is no doubt as to the genuineness of the dial, and the aspect is due south. Now, what can be found out from these facts ? Examine the records of Experimental Dial No. I on p. 55, which, like the Kilmersdon one, faces due south, and has a horizontal style. It will be seen that the angles which the shadow makes throughout the year at 9 a.m. vary. In the winter the angles formed are about 9° or 10°, at the equinoxes about 33°, and in the summer about 49°.[1]

---

[1] These figures do not quite agree with those given on p. 55, but it has been explained that the numbers there given are taken from about the middle of each month. The figures given above are taken from the full records.

The shadow never approaches nearer the vertical line than the angle 49°.

Turning now to the photo of the dial at Kilmersdon and measuring the angles, it is seen that the noon-line makes an angle of 90°, and the other line, the one stated to be at about 9 a.m., is at an angle of 60° or 62°.

Compare these lines, at angles of 49° and 60°, on the Standard Dial, and it will be seen that it is absolutely impossible for the sun to cast a shadow at 9 a.m. *during any period of the year* on the line marked at an angle of 60° on the dial at Kilmersdon.

Obviously there is a mistake here : either the dial does not face due south or the theory is at fault.

Incidentally it may be noted that the position of the line at 60° is very different from that of the figure VIII on a clock-face which is placed at the angle 30°.

It may be argued that the time for Mass varied, and that at this church it was fixed for 10 a.m. The full records of Dial I show that the shadow does fall on the line 60° from May to about the end of July, and so the Kilmersdon dial would mark a 10 a.m. Mass-time correctly at midsummer, but in midwinter this 10 a.m. Mass would be before 8 o'clock.

The Kilmersdon dial may be looked at from another point of view. Suppose the maker of the dial said, " Mass is said at 9 a.m. I will use this line (60°) to mark that time—that is, when the shadow falls on this line, then is the correct time to say Mass."

If he proceeded in this way he would have his service

In January	about 11.15 a.m.	In August	about 10.20 a.m.
,, February	,, 11 a.m.	,, September	,, 10.40 a.m.
,, March	,, 10.50 a.m.	,, October	,, 10.50 a.m.
,, April	,, 10.30 a.m.	,, November	,, 11.0 a.m.
,, May, June, July	,, 10.0 a.m.	,, December	,, 11.20 a.m.

Thus the 9 a.m. Mass would take place at this church

at times varying from about 10 to 11.20. This seems absurd, for in midwinter it would be nearly 2½ hours late.

This is the first dial illustrated in Fr. Horne's book with a definite Mass-line.

The next one, Portbury, also faces due south, and the Mass-line is placed at an angle of 54°. This is very similar to the first one, and no shadow could possibly fall on this line at 9 a.m. at any period of the year.

There is one other dial, illustrated on p. 46, at Baltonsborough, which also faces due south, and may conveniently be considered here. The Mass-line on this is at an angle of 45°, so this dial would have a shadow on it or near it in the summer, viz. from the beginning of May till the end of June, at about 9 a.m., but in the winter the shadow would not be on it much before 11 a.m.

Again, take the dial at Stratton-on-the-Fosse, illustrated on p. 24,[1] which faces S. 3° W. The Mass-line is described as sharp and distinct, and it is at an angle of about 40°. There is no Experimental Dial facing exactly S. 3° W., but Dial I shows a difference of only 3°, and it is probable this Mass-line would have a shadow on it at about 10.30 in the winter, instead of at 9 a.m.

The dial at Rempton, illustrated on p. 64,[1] faces S. 15° E., and the Mass-line here makes an angle of 58°. This may be compared with Experimental Dial No. V, which has the same aspect, and the records of this dial show that at no period of the year could there possibly be a shadow on this line at 9 a.m.

The dial at White Lackington, illustrated on p. 70,[1] faces S. 20° E. It is a hole-dial, and the Mass-line is referred to as duplicated, that is, there are 2 holes marking it. This line is at 20°. There is no Experimental Dial just like this, but by comparing the records

[1] In Fr. Horne's book.

of Dials V and VI, which face S. 15° E. and S. 30° E.,
it is probable that there would be a shadow on this
Mass-line before 7 a.m. in July and before 9 a.m. in
midwinter.

These are the six Mass-clocks illustrated in Fr.
Horne's book which have well-marked Mass-lines on
their faces, and from a consideration of them in conjunction with the records of the absolute position of the
shadow as seen on the various Experimental Dials at
varying periods throughout the year, the conclusion is
forced upon one that not one of these dials, if fitted with
a gnomon at right angles to its plane, would be of the
slightest use as a correct time-marker for the service of
Mass.

The suggestion that the Mass-line corresponds with
the position of the figure VIII on a clock-face is also
found not to be always correct, for VIII on a clock is
fixed at an angle of 30°, whereas the Mass-lines vary in
the angles they form from 20° to 60°.

Having examined these photographs, let us return to
Fr. Horne's theory as I have ventured to state it.

1. It may at once be acceded that one of the principal
uses of these dials, and probably the most important,
was to mark the time of Mass ; but if they also served
as general time-tellers, they would still, and in no less
degree, serve as Mass-markers. It is possible that the
person who made the most use of a dial was the bell-
ringer. His duty was to call the people to church at the
right time, and it is reasonable to suppose that he would
find a dial very useful.

2. If the angles which the Mass-lines form, as seen on
dials, be measured, they will be found to vary considerably. Those in Fr. Horne's book vary from 20° to
60°, and an angle of about 45° may be taken as a very
common one. *But* a dial having a Mass-line at 45°

and a *horizontal* style would register about 2 hours wrong in the winter.

Taking a dial facing due south and having a horizontal style, the best angle for the Mass-line is 33°. This is supposing the simplest kind of dial, i.e. a dial with only one line to mark the time of Mass approximately all the year round. On such a dial the shadow will fall on the line 33° twice a year at 9 a.m., viz. at the two equinoxes, but as midsummer and midwinter are approached, the time of course becomes more and more inaccurate.

3. That a dial fitted with a style at right angles to its plane is not a correct time-teller is amply proved by an examination of the records of the Experimental Dials, but the same examination will conclusively show that, fitted with styles bent at appropriate angles, the dial can be made to tell the correct time with a very fair degree of accuracy, a degree of accuracy which would be amply sufficient.

4. It has been shown on pp. 85–87 that the dials at Kilmersdon, Portbury and Rempton would, *if fitted with horizontal styles*, never have a shadow on their Mass-lines at 9 a.m. at any period of the year, and in the other cases the times registered would be so inaccurate as to be absolutely useless.

It is possible Fr. Horne has not stated the facts about the dials with accuracy. For instance, he may, when stating the aspect of a dial, have omitted to allow for the variation of the compass, etc.

5. It is here that Fr. Horne has fallen into an error, but in this he has only followed the example set him by everyone who has written on this subject; for, while admitting that a horizontal style will give but inaccurate results, they all insist that it must have been this variety which was used. No reason for this universal opinion has ever been produced.

Once it is recognized that the style used was not always at right angles to the plane of the dial, but that it might be varied to suit different orientations of the dial and different periods of the year, by being bent in such a manner as always to point due south and when necessary to an angle which was less than a right angle, then all the various difficulties disappear.

For if a dial possesses such a style or styles, the question of the exact angle formed by the Mass-line does not matter, it is just a detail which can be adjusted, and there will be no dial upon the Mass-line of which the sun cannot cast a shadow at every period of the year. Dials made in this manner are capable of being real time-markers, and telling the correct time are thus Mass-markers and service-markers, no matter what hour was chosen for holding such services.

Mr. George F. J. Rosenberg, of King's School, Canterbury, has, in a lecture delivered before the local Archæological Society, propounded a most ingenious theory. In reply to a letter asking for information, he has, with a kindness for which I am very grateful, forwarded me a copy of his lecture, with the photographs and diagrams illustrating it. It is to be hoped he will publish his views in a more extended form, and so enable everyone interested in the subject to understand his point of view.

Mr. Rosenberg accepts unquestioned the position of the style as being at right angles to the plane of the dial. It is not thus stated in his paper, but it may reasonably be inferred. Having the great advantage of being a mathematician, he has worked out the position of the shadow on dials at different times and at different seasons and for different orientations. He believes these dials marked the times of the service of Mass, but he does not restrict this time to any particular hour, but he mentions various times about 9 or 10 a.m. or between these hours.

He also considers the dials frequently mark the noon-hour, but he by no means considers the vertical line on a dial to be always or generally the noon-line.

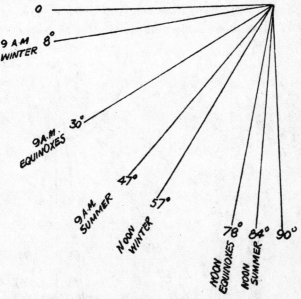

0

9 A·M 8°
WINTER

9 A.M 30°
EQUINOXES

9 A.M 45°
SUMMER

NOON 57°
WINTER

78° 84° 90°

NOON NOON
EQUINOXES SUMMER

MR. ROSENBERG'S DIAGRAM FOR DIALS FACING S. 10° W.

Perhaps the theory may be best explained by taking an example.

One of the dials worked out by Mr. Rosenberg is the upper of the three dials on the east of the south doorway at Barfreston (see Plate I, No. 4). It faces rather less than S. 10° W.

There are five lines on this dial, and the upper three are supposed to mark 9 a.m., the top one for three months in winter, the middle one for three months at each equinox, and the lower one for three months in the summer.

A diagram is given (which is copied on p. 91) of the correct position of the shadows on a dial facing S. 10° W. at those various times with the vertical and horizontal lines 90° and 0°.

The dial No. 4 at Barfreston has all the appearance of being well cut, but when examined carefully the two upper lines are seen to curve, and there is no horizontal line. There is also considerable doubt as to the vertical

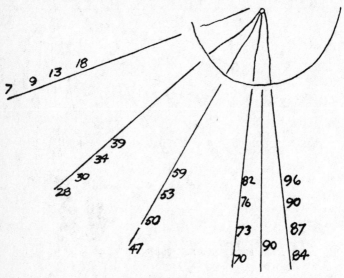

BARFRESTON NO. 4.

line. It would seem that there is no vertical line drawn, but its place is taken by a small hole about half-way between the two last lines on the right-hand side. A line drawn through this hole would probably be strictly vertical, the right-hand (E) line on the dial not being truly vertical but inclining at its lower end to the right or east. A tracing of the dial is given here with extended lines, the angles being measured from four different starting-points.

It may be interesting first of all to compare the dial with the Standard Dial, and for this we will take a line through the hole already mentioned and treat that as the vertical line, thus :

Hours	.	.	VI	VII	VIII		IX	X	XI		XII	I
Standard	.	.	0°	15°	30°		45°	60°	75°		90°	105°
Barfreston No. 4 .			18°		39°		59°			82°	(90)°	96°

Now compare the dial with Mr. Rosenberg's diagram. Suppose, firstly, that the right-hand line is taken as being vertical at 90° :

	9 a.m., Winter.	9 a.m., Equinoxes.	9 a.m., Summer.	Noon, Winter.	Noon, Equinoxes.	Noon, Summer.
Mr. Rosenberg's Diagram .	8°	30°	47°	57°	78°	84°
Barfreston No. 4	13°	34°	53°		76°	90°

Mr. Rosenberg considers this dial " an extraordinarily well and accurately drawn dial," marking by its upper three lines 9 a.m. (the time of Mass) in the winter, at the two equinoxes and in the summer. The two other lines he considers " are clearly a winter and summer noon-line, though not placed quite as accurately."

There is no doubt that the lines at 13° and 34° are fairly correctly placed for 9 o'clock in the summer and at the equinoxes, but the line 53° is more nearly noon in winter than 9 in summer. The lines 76° and 90° may be taken to mark noon at the equinoxes and in summer.

But it has to be borne in mind that on a dial S. 10° W., with a style at right angles to the plane of the dial, the shadow *must* be to the west (left) of the vertical at noon in the summer. This is shown by Mr. Rosenberg's diagram, where it is seen to be at 84°, whereas the right-hand line at Barfreston is almost certainly to the east of vertical. This fact seems to present an insuperable objection to its representing the position of the shadow at noon in the summer.

The angles on this dial may be measured in another

way. It may be argued that the most important lines
are the three left-hand ones, and if you place the protractor so that the angle 30° exactly corresponds with the
middle one of these lines, the following result is obtained
(it hardly seems, by the by, a fair way to proceed) :

	9 a.m., Winter.	9 a.m., Equinoxes.	9 a.m., Summer.	Noon, Winter.	Noon, Equinoxes.	Noon, Summer.
Diagram . .	8°	30°	47°	57°	78°	84°
Barfreston .	9°	30°	50°		73°	87°

This gives a fairly accurate result, but it has only been
obtained by placing the protractor in a tilted position,
for the angle, which now measures 87° and is to the west
of vertical, should really measure 96° and be to the east
of vertical.

A fourth way of measuring the angles on this dial may
be given. Mr. Rosenberg considers the right-hand line
to mark noon in summer, and his diagram gives the
angle for this time as 84°. If, therefore, you place the
84° line of the protractor over this right-hand line this
result is obtained:

	9 a.m., Winter.	9 a.m., Equinoxes.	9 a.m., Summer.	Noon, Winter.	Noon, Equinoxes.	Noon, Summer.
Diagram . .	8°	30°	47°	57°	78°	84°
Barfreston .	7°	28°	47°		70°	84°

The result seems to be excellent, but the same objection can be advanced as in the last case ; but here the
tilting of the protractor has had to be carried farther,
and the line 84°, which should be on the left of the vertical,
now measures 96°, and is on the right of the vertical line.

Every endeavour has been made to accommodate this
dial to Mr. Rosenberg's theory, but the fatal objection
is that in summer the noon-line, on a dial facing S. 10° W.
and with a style at right angles to the plane of the dial,
must be to the *west* of vertical, and this dial has this
easterly line to the east of vertical. To overcome this
objection is not to adjust an inaccuracy, it is to achieve

the impossible. This one line being proved to be wrong, all the seeming accuracy of the other lines is upset.[1]

According to Mr. Rosenberg's theory, dials facing south or west of south should have all their lines in the left-hand (west) lower quadrant, and the position of the lowest line must be either vertical at 90° or at an angle less than 90°.[2] If on dials oriented in this manner there are lines on the right-hand side, then their use is not explained by this theory. The writer's note-books contain (leaving out a number of doubtful dials), photos or sketches of thirty-eight dials with the above-named aspects, all of which show lines on the right-hand side, i.e. in the lower east quadrant. An inquirer may quite properly ask, What are these lines for?

The same note-books contain photos or sketches (leaving out doubtful ones) of thirteen dials on walls facing south or west of south, which have lines or holes on the left *only*, that is, in the left (west) lower quadrant.

It seems reasonable to suggest that among dials such as these, confirmation or otherwise of this theory might be most expected to be found.

LIST OF DIALS FACING S. OR S.W. WHICH HAVE LINES OR HOLES ONLY IN THE LEFT (WEST) LOWER QUADRANT.[3]

Barfreston Nos. 1, 3, 4, 6, 8. Aspect S. 10° W.
Burghclere Nos. 1, 5   „   S.
Herriard Nos. 1, 4, 7   „   S.
Stoke Charity Nos. 1, 3   „   S.
Timsbury, one   „   S.

It seems to be giving the theory every chance if dials from this list be compared with Mr. Rosenberg's diagram.

---

[1] This dial is analysed on p. 105.

[2] See diagram, *ante*, p. 91.

[3] It may be remarked that these thirteen dials are all on five churches, and it would seem that this particular variety is more generally found on those churches which possess numerous dials.

In order to do this, tracings have been made from photographs, and then, the lines having been extended, the angles were measured.

DIAL No. 3 AT BARFRESTON COMPARED WITH MR. ROSENBERG'S DIAGRAM, P. 91.

Aspect, S. 10° W.

		9 a.m., Winter.	9 a.m., Equin.	9 am., Summer.	Noon, Winter.	Noon, Equin.	Noon, Summer.	
Diagram, p. 91	0°	8°	30°	47°	57°	78°	84°	90°
Barfreston [1]	0°		25°	41°	57°	72°	83°	90°

[1] For tracing of dial and other particulars, see Analysis of Dials, p. 104. For photo see Plate I.

Mr. Rosenberg considers this dial marks three Mass-lines, one for winter, one for the two equinoxes and one for the summer; and two noon-lines, more accurately placed than on Dial 4 at Barfreston. The enlarged tracing seems to show the three noon-lines placed with a very considerable degree of accuracy, leaving two other lines, neither of which is very accurate, for 9 a.m. at the equinoxes and 9 a.m. in the summer.

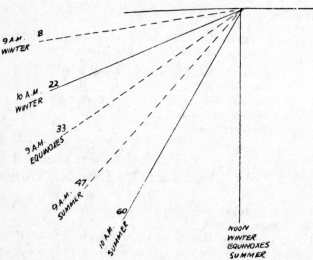

MR. ROSENBERG'S DIAGRAM FOR DIALS FACING DUE SOUTH.

DIAL NO. 5 AT BURGHCLERE COMPARED WITH MR. ROSENBERG'S DIAGRAM.

Aspect, due south.

	9 a.m., Winter.	9 a.m., Equinoxes.	9 a.m., Summer.	Noon, Winter, Equinoxes, Summer.
Diagram, p. 96	8°	33°	47°	90°
Burghclere [1] .		38°		

[1] For tracing, etc., see Analysis of Dials, p. 113.

This dial seems to have only one line, and the best angle for it, according to this theory, would be at 33° to mark 9 a.m. at the equinoxes.

DIAL NO. 1 AT HERRIARD COMPARED WITH MR. ROSENBERG'S DIAGRAM.

Aspect, due south.

	9 a.m., Winter.	9 a.m., Equinoxes.	9 a.m., Summer.	10 a.m., Summer.		Noon.
Diagram, p. 96 .	8°	33°	47°	60°		90°
Herriard No. 1. [1]				62°	76°	90°

[1] For tracing, etc., see Analysis of Dials, p. 119.

This does not seem to support the theory at all.

DIAL NO. 4 AT HERRIARD COMPARED WITH MR. ROSENBERG'S DIAGRAM.

Aspect, due south.

	9 a.m., Winter.	10 a.m., Winter.	9 a.m., Equin.	9 a.m., Summer.	10 a.m., Summer.		Noon, Winter, Equin., Summer.
Diagram, p. 96 .	8°	22°	33°	47°	60°		90°
Herriard No. 4 [1]			32°	48°	60°	76°	90°

[1] For tracing, etc., see Analysis of Dials, p. 121.

This would be correct for 9 a.m. at the equinoxes and in the summer. It would also be right for 10 a.m. in the summer, and of course it would be correct for noon all the year round. It could not be wrong for the latter.

This is wonderfully correct, but why should there be two lines for the summer, one at 9 a.m. and the other at 10 a.m. ? If it was for the winter Mass one could understand its being an hour later.

The theory offers no explanation for the line at 76°.

DIAL No. 3 AT STOKE CHARITY COMPARED WITH MR. ROSENBERG'S DIAGRAM.

Aspect, due south.

	9 a.m., Winter.	10 a.m. Winter.	9 a.m., Equin.	9 a.m., Summer.	10 a.m. Summer.	Noon, Winter, Equin., Summer.
Diagram, p. 96	8°	22°	33°	47°	60°	90°
Stoke Charity [1]			28°	41° 56°		78° 90°

[1] For tracing, etc., see Analysis of Dials, p. 137.

This is not very accurate, but it might be taken to mark 9 a.m. at the equinoxes and in the summer and 10 a.m. in the summer.

The theory offers no explanation of the line 78°.

DIAL AT TIMSBURY COMPARED WITH MR. ROSENBERG'S DIAGRAM.

Aspect, due south.

	9 a.m., Winter.	10 a.m. Winter.	9 a.m., Equin.	9 p.m., Summer.	10 a.m., Summer.	Noon, Winter, Equin., Summer.
Diagram, p. 96 .	8°	22°	33°	47°	60°	90°
Timsbury [1] .			28°		49° 74°	90°

[1] For tracing, etc., see Analysis of Dials, p. 138.

This does not seem to support the theory.

Perhaps this dial should not be included in this list, as it is not certain if the line on the right which has been taken at 90° is strictly vertical.

Mr. Rosenberg's theory, of which only a brief account has been given, has been tested at some length, not only because it is a very ingenious and attractive one, but also because he himself says that " the strongest test of the accuracy of the theory lies in the numerous cases where the lines are extremely accurately placed in accordance with it." Its truth or otherwise must be left to the investigation of observers in various parts of the country.

The following criticisms may be permitted.

1. None of the lines, however accurately placed, would

give the correct time either for 9 a.m. or, generally, for noon for more than a few days, each line only pretending to a fairly average approximation of the correct time round about four fixed dates. This is unfortunate, especially in the case of the correct time for noon, for by a most simple device [1] noon can be found on any dial, however oriented, with absolute accuracy for every day in the year, and that with the use of one line only and not three.

2. The theory ignores altogether the well-marked Mass-line which is a distinct feature of many dials, so much a feature, in fact, that Fr. Horne considers that it is "alone the line for which the dial was usually constructed."

3. The theory fails to explain a very large number of dials, a number which is far in excess of those which it can by any possibility hope to explain. Take, for instance, the wheel dials or even the half-wheel dials, the latter having, when fully developed, thirteen lines, whereas only six are accounted for by the three 9 a.m. lines and the three noon-lines.

Mr. Rosenberg has evidently foreseen this difficulty, and has endeavoured to explain it by suggesting that the wheel dials were not used for any purpose after being built into the wall, but were equatorial dials. He says : " Such markings are exactly what would be needed for equatorial dials, and it is my belief that when the church was being built, a stone, or perhaps in some cases a piece of wood, was so marked and used as an equatorial dial for determining by observation the correct position of the shadow lines on the dial which was eventually scratched on the vertical wall of the church." The stone, being valuable as building material, was not wasted, but built into the wall of the church.

[1] See Chapter V, p. 66.

Now, an equatorial dial is one the plane of which is at right angles to the style and therefore parallel to the equator. On it is a circle, divided into twenty-four equal hour divisions. The style must point accurately to the north pole and the noon division must coincide with the meridian plane. If all these conditions are complied with, the shadow will tell the sun time accurately.

It may well be asked, Was it possible for the makers of the dials we are considering, say the parish priest or sexton, to make an equatorial dial ? It is not quite an easy thing to do nowadays, when one may avoid having to find the meridian plane by setting the style by Greenwich Time, making due allowance for longitude and for the Equation of Time. Could you find in country villages to-day many parish priests or sextons who would undertake to make an equatorial dial ? It seems almost certain that the answer to these questions must be in the negative. The difficulties raised by this point are practically insuperable.

But suppose, for the sake of argument, it is allowed that equatorial dials were made, say one for each church throughout the land. Each church then possessed an excellent time-marker, so why proceed further ? The object is attained. If the second dial you are going to make by the aid of the equatorial dial is to be a better one, well and good ; but the second dial proves, on examination, to be only a makeshift ; it will only give you the time, and that inaccurately, round about 9 a.m. and noon at certain periods of the year. There are certain disadvantages attaching to equatorial dials ; they are more exposed to the influence of the weather, and they must be set up at some distance from churches, houses, trees, etc., in order that the shadow may not be obstructed ; but apart from these limitations, and they could both be easily overcome, the equatorial dials are infinitely more useful and more accurate than scratch dials.

The theory, then, is incapable of explaining the use of a very large number of dials, and it brings to its aid, to account for these, a sub-theory which is very difficult of acceptance.

It is easy to bring forward objections, but, after all, the theory must stand or fall by the number of dials which can be found which accurately conform with it.

It is possible, upon further investigation, that it may be found to explain the use of a certain number of dials while not pretending to account for all dials.

No very definite date can be given as to when sundials were first constructed in England on scientific principles. We know that they were in use in the sixteenth century and that they were becoming common in the seventeenth century, and it is certain that their construction was known at an earlier period.

That being so, another theory which has been advanced to explain Mass-clocks is that they were constructed on scientific principles, although perhaps not very accurately. To make a scientific dial, the gnomon must point due south, and must incline to the horizontal at an angle equal to the latitude of the place. The correct position of the lines on the dial has then to be found, the graduations of which differ according to the orientation of the dial.

Thus on a dial facing due south the lines should be at the following angles [1] :

Hours	VI	VII	VIII	IX	X	XI	XII	I	II	III	IV	V	VI
	0°	23°	43°	58°	70°	80°	90°	100°	110°	122°	137°	157°	180°

A dial such as this is practically the same as the one

---

[1] These figures were worked out mathematically for me by Captain J. G. Green, R.N.

constructed from the records of my Experimental Dial No. X.[1]

On dials facing east or west of south the position of the lines would be different in every case.

In the light of our present knowledge we may say that the makers of the dials we are considering *ought* to have constructed them in this manner, but that they *did* do so is more than doubtful.

The writer has been so fortunate as to have worked out for him [2] the exact position which the lines should occupy on a large number of dials facing to the east and to the west of south, and he has compared these with the position of the lines on actual dials, and having examined a large number of these dials, and taking account of the orientation of each, he is obliged to confess that he has failed to find any agreement whatsoever between them.

Sometimes a dial can be found on which the lines are cut at the correct angles but the orientation of the dial is wrong. For instance, Dial No. 4 at Herriard is a case in point.

Hours . . .	VII	VIII	IX	X	XI	XII	
Herriard No. 4 [3] .	32°	48°	60°	76°		90°	
The angles should be	32½°	48°	60½°	72°	80½°	90°	on a dial S. 10° W.

These angles seem very accurate, 76° standing for 10.30 a.m.; but unfortunately this dial does not face S. 10° W., but exactly due south.

Numerous other similar instances could be given, but not one dial has been found by the writer to show that the ordinary Mass-clock was constructed and used as a scientifically made sundial.

[1] See Chapter VI, p. 74.
[2] By Captain J. G. Green, R.N.
[3] See Analysis of Dials, p. 121.

CHAPTER IX

ANALYSIS OF DIALS

To obtain a true idea of a dial, a more correct appreciation than is obtained by simply looking at it, it is necessary to measure the angles which the lines or holes form. It is surprising how different a dial appears when submitted to this test. The method adopted here to measure the angles is to make an accurate tracing of the photograph or enlarged photograph of a dial and then carefully to extend the lines. Having done this, the protractor enables the lines to have placed upon them the number or degree representing the angles they form. These angles can then be compared with the angles on a Standard Dial, made after the pattern of a compass. Strict accuracy is not claimed for this method, but it certainly gives a much truer idea of a dial than is obtained by mere inspection.

The dials of which analyses are given in the following pages have not been selected because they happen to suit this theory or that, but the choice has in the main depended upon the possibility of making an accurate tracing. The chief fact which emerges from a review of these analyses is that the angles which the lines or holes form on the great majority of dials are 15° or multiples of 15° apart. This is seen to be the case over and over again. Details are given in Chapter V which demonstrate that dials made on this plan can be made very efficient time-markers.

LIST OF DIALS ANALYSED

Barfreston, Kent, Nos. 3, 4, 5, 7.

Bishop's Sutton No. 3.

Bramley Nos. 3, 4.

Burghclere Nos. 2, 4, 5, 7.

Chaddesley Nos. 2, 3.

Downton.

Hayling, South, No. 1.

Herriard Nos. 1, 2, 3, 4, 5, 6.

Laverstoke.

Martin Nos. 3, 4.

Martley.

Penton Mewsey.

Salisbury, St. Martin's.

Sherborne St. John Nos. 1, 3.

Steventon No. 2.

Stoke Charity Nos. 3, 6.

Timsbury.

Up Nateley.

Warnford No. 1.

The numbers are those given in Chapter X.

Barfreston Dial, No. 3. Aspect, S. 10° W.

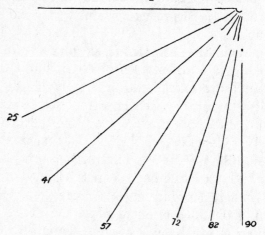

BARFRESTON NO. 3. WEDGE-SHAPED.

Hours		VI	VII	VIII	IX	X	XI	XII
Standard		0°	15°	30°	45°	60°	75°	90°
Barfreston	(a)			25°	41°	57°	72°	82°
	(b)			28°	44°	60°	75°	85°

This peculiar dial has wedge-shaped lines, and the angles (*a*) given above are those at the bottom (centre) of the wide wedge. It is possible that the right-hand (east) edge of each mark was used to denote the hours, and if so, the angles ought to be advanced several degrees.

If 3° are added (*b*), the result compares very accurately with the angles on the Standard Dial.

Noon was probably marked by the hole seen outside the circular line.

Used in this manner and with styles bent to face due south and also bent down at appropriate angles, this dial would be an excellent time-marker.

See illustration, Plate I, and description, p. 185.

Barfreston No. 4.   Aspect, S. 10° W.

This has the appearance of a well-cut dial, but when examined carefully the two upper lines are seen to curve and the vertical line is not truly vertical.

The reader is referred to the Chapter on " Various Theories," pp. 91–94, where a diagram is given and the dial is analysed according to Mr. Rosenberg's theory.

Here the dial will be analysed quite differently, according to the " bent style theory."

The right-hand line is taken as the starting-point, and the results are :

Hours	.	.	VI	VII	VIII	IX	X	XI	XII
Standard	.	.	0°	15°	30°	45°	60°	75°	90°
Barfreston	.			13°	34°		53°		76°	90°

This seems, in all probability, the way in which this dial was used, but it may be pointed out that to obtain this result, viz. that the shadow should fall on the line 90°, which really slants to the east at its lower part, the style could not have been at right angles to the plane of the dial, but must have been bent slightly to the east, i.e. it must have pointed due south.

Probably the intention of the maker was to mark 7, 8, 9.30, and 11 and noon; but the two upper lines are uncertain ones, and it is difficult to understand why they are present, for if the table [1] on p. 82 be referred to, it will be seen that on a dial facing S. 10° W. there is never a shadow at 7 a.m., and probably only at certain periods of the year would there be a shadow at 8 or 8.30 a.m.

This dial furnishes a good example of the deceptiveness of dials ; at first sight it looks an excellent one, but when its several parts are analysed, it proves to be far from accurate.

See illustration, Plate I, and description, p. 185.

Barfreston No. 5 (the middle dial).   Aspect, S. 10° W.

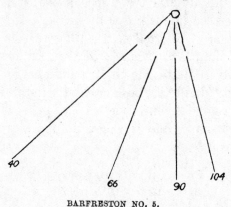

BARFRESTON NO. 5.

This dial has four lines, and a horizontal one through the style-hole may be considered to be formed by the edge of the stone.

Hours			VI	VII	VIII	IX	X	XI	XII	I
Standard	.		0°	15°	30°	45°	60°	75°	90°	105°
Barfreston	.					40°	66°		90°	104°

It seems to be intended to mark the hours 9, 10, 12 and 1, and if so it must have had a style, not at right

---

[1] Chapter VII.

angles to its plane, but pointing due south or nearly so, as the second line from the right is nearly vertical.

It does not correspond with Mr. Rosenberg's diagram for S. 10° W., and is not mentioned by him.

See illustration, Plate I, and description, p. 185.

Barfreston No. 7. A complete wheel. Aspect, S. 10° W.

This may be considered a perfect dial, the angles all being 15° apart.

Hours	.	VI	VII	VIII	IX	X	XI	XII	I	II	III	IV	V		VI
Standard	.	0°	15°	30°	45°	60°	75°	90°	105°	120°	135°	150°	165°		180°
Barfreston, Lower half		0°	14°	30°	45°	60°	75°	90°	105°	120°	135°	150°	162°	170°	180°
Barfreston, Top	.		15°	30°	45°	60°	74°	91°	104°	119°	134°	149°	162°		180°

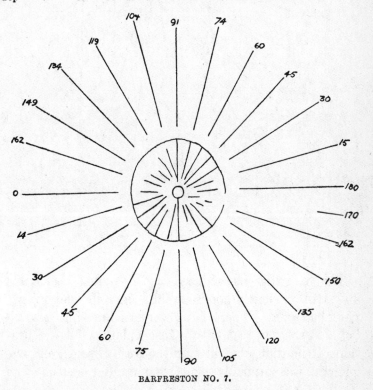

BARFRESTON NO. 7.

The line marked 170° on the right is very short, and perhaps forms no part of the dial; but it is just here where the only error in the dial occurs, for the next line should be 165° and not 162°.

Note.—The 10 a.m. line is continued outside the circle, and ends in a small hole.

See illustration, Plate I, and description, p. 186.

Bishop's Sutton No. 3.   Aspect, S. 2° or 3° W.

Hours	VI	VII	VIII	IX	X	XI	XII	I	II	III	IV	V	VI
Standard	0°	15°	30°	45°	60°	75°	90°	105°	120°	135°	150°	165°	180°
Bishop's Sutton		14°	29°	40°	46°	59°	79°	90°	95°	106°	125°	145°	155°

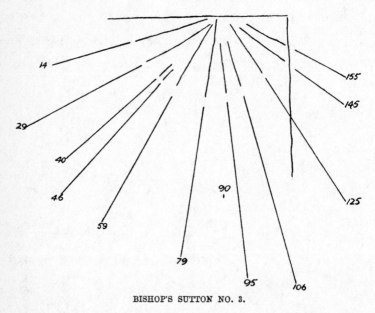

BISHOP'S SUTTON NO. 3.

The following particulars may be noted. The line 29° is an extremely good one, and lines 40° and 46° are very bad ones. There is no vertical line, but a small hole is probably meant to take its place. The orientation of the dial is slightly to the west of south and the gnomon was probably bent to point due south. The

lines 14°, 29°, 46°, 59°, 90° and 106° are very accurate.
The line 40° probably marks 8.30, 79° = 11.30, 95° =
12.30. Line 125° may mark 2 or 2.30, 145° = 3.30 and
155° = 4.30.

See illustration, Plate IX, and description, p. 143.

Bramley No. 3.   Aspect, due south.

Hours .		VII	IX	X	XI	XII	I	II	III	IV
Standard	.	30°	45°	60°	75°	90°	105°	120°	135°	150°
Bramley	.		44°	59°	75°	95°	105°		128°	140°

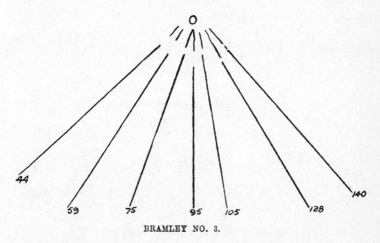

BRAMLEY NO. 3.

There are seven lines on this dial, not one of which
passes through the centre of the style-hole. Of these
lines, the five on the right are cut on the right of the
style-hole, while the two on the left are cut on the left
of the style-hole. From this cause the vertical line is
not at 90° but at 95°, and noon, to be correct, would
be marked when the right-hand side of the shadow
reached this line. The hours 9 to 1 are correctly
marked, and the lines marking 11 and 1 are especially
accurate. The two lines on the right are not good ones,
but perhaps they are intended to mark 2.30 and 3.30.

It seems to have been a badly constructed dial, and has been much damaged by scraping.

See illustration, Plate IV, and description, p. 144.

Bramley No. 5.   Aspect, due south.

Hours .		VI	VII		VIII	IX	X	XI	XII		I	II	III		IV		V
Standard	.	0°	15°		30°	45°	60°	75°	90°		105°	120°	135°		150°		165°
Bramley	.			22°		43°	59°	76°	90°	97°	107°	120°		141°		158°

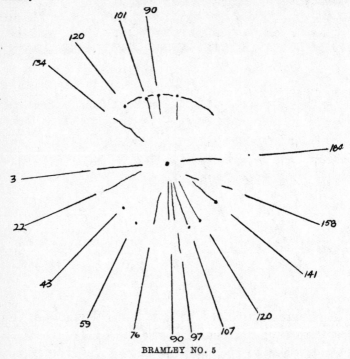

BRAMLEY NO. 5

A very correct analysis of this dial is not possible, for the style-hole is blocked and many of the lines are destroyed by scraping and cement. Another difficulty is that the vertical and horizontal lines do not form accurate right angles.

The tracing is from an enlarged photograph.

The line which appears to slope a little to the west at the lower end is taken as the vertical line, and it should be noted that there are only two well-marked lines now present. They no doubt mark 1 and 2 o'clock.

The analysis shows that the hours 9 to 2 are correct. Line 22° may mark 7.30, that is, the time half-way between 6 and 9 a.m. Line 97°, which is not very clear, may mark 12.30, and lines 141° and 158° may mark 3.30 and 4.30.

See illustration, Plate IV, and description, p. 145.

Burghclere No. 2. On east jamb of south doorway. Aspect, due south.

An imperfect dial. The small hole below the stylehole may not mark noon. If it does, the one line really to be seen plainly is at 32°, which corresponds to Rosenberg's 9 a.m. line at the equinoxes, which is 33°. Then there are two holes below and to the right of the stylehole. Have these any connection with the dial ?

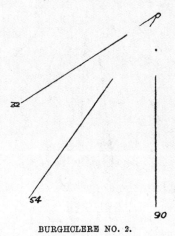

BURGHCLERE NO. 2.

This dial is rather like the one on the west jamb of the same doorway, and if they marked the time of Mass, the east jamb dial is at 32° and the west jamb dial at 38°.

For illustration, see Plate III, and description, p. 146.

Burghclere No. 4. West jamb of south doorway. Aspect, due south.

This is a dial of the wheel type, but has some peculiarities, for the vertical lines do not form exact right angles with the horizontal lines and several lines are absent.

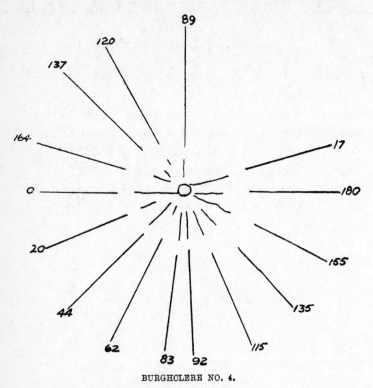

BURGHCLERE NO. 4.

In the lower half the angles are :

Hours	VI	VII	7.30	VIII	IX	X	XI	11.30	XII	I	1.30	II	III	IV	4.30	V	VI
Standard	0°	15°		30°	45°	60°	75°		90°	105°		120°	135°	150°		165°	180°
Burghclere	0°		20°		44°	62°		83°	92°		115°		135°		155°		180°

From this we see that the three-hourly divisions, 6, 9, 12, 3 and 6, are marked with much accuracy, and then three of these divisions are halved, but not quite so correctly. Thus 7.30 (half-way between 6 and 9) should be 22½°, 1.30 should be 112½° and 4.30 should be 157½°.

Ten o'clock is nearly correct, and 11.30, marked by 83°, should be 82½°. It is not apparent why the angles should be so irregular, but taking a broad view, it seems reasonable to suppose that the construction aimed at was a dial having lines 15° apart or 15° + (half) 7½°.

For illustration, see Plate II, and description, p. 147.

Burghclere No. 5. On west jamb of south doorway. Aspect, due south.

The upper line seems to slant upwards, but it forms a right angle with the hole which marks noon.

This is a real Mass-clock, there being only one

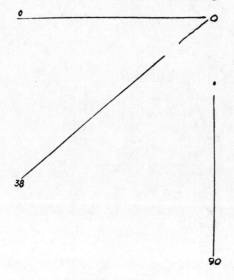

BURGHCLERE NO. 5.

line. This line is at the angle 38°. It does not correspond with any of Mr. Rosenberg's lines, the nearest being 9 a.m. at the equinoxes, which is 33°.

Probably this dial had bent-down styles, and marked

the time for the service of Mass all the year round, or it may have been used in conjunction with Dial No. 2 (see *ante*), one for the summer and the other for the winter.

For illustration, see Plate II, and description, p. 147.

Burghclere No. 7.   South-east angle of nave.   Aspect, S. 8° E.

This is a most interesting wheel dial with very accurate lines.

Hours	. VI (6.30)	VII	VIII	IX	X	XI	XII	I	II	(2.30)	III	IV	V	VI
Standard	0°		15°	30°	45°	60°	75°	90°	105°	120°		135°	150°	165°	180°
Burghclere	8°			29°	46°	62°	75°	90°	107°		128°		151°	167°	180°

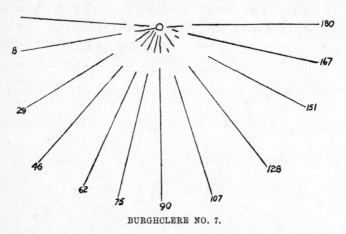

BURGHCLERE NO. 7.

It will be observed that the hours 8 to 1 inclusive are practically correct, as are also the hours 4, 5 and 6.

The hours 6 and 7 a.m. and 2 and 3 p.m. are not marked, but the time between each is halved very accurately, 8° standing for 6.30 and 128° for 2.30. This latter line, it may be noted, is a very distinct one. The top line on the left (west) side is not easy to explain, for although this dial faces S. 8° E. and so gets the sun on it earlier than a dial facing due south, yet a reference to the Table on p. 82 will show that even on a dial (No. V) facing S. 15° E. there is never a shadow at 6 a.m., and this top line slants upwards and might be expected to mark a time antecedent to 6 o'clock.

It may, however, be noted, as showing how regularly the lines on this dial are spaced at distances of $7\frac{1}{2}°$ and 15°, that even this top line is 14° from the one next to it.

Referring again to the line 8°, which possibly marks 6.30 a.m., it seems probable, taking into account the orientation of the dial, that this would be about the time when at certain periods of the year a shadow would first fall on this dial.

For illustration, see Plate III; for description, see p. 147.

Chaddesley Corbett No. 2.   Aspect, S. 10° E.

This dial has some faint lines on the west side, but these cannot be traced.   The lines on the east are quite clearly cut.

Hours	XII	I	II	III	IV
Standard	90°	105°	120°	135°	150°
Chaddesley	90°	104°	116°	131°	148°

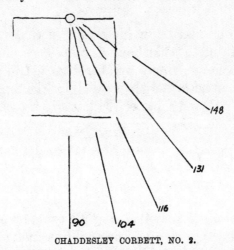

CHADDESLEY CORBETT, NO. 2.

Here the lines mark fairly accurately the hours 12 to 4. For illustration, see Plate IV; for description, see p. 189.

Chaddesley Corbett No. 3. Dial with Roman numbers. Aspect, S. 10° E.

A tracing of this dial with lines extended shows the following angles.

Hours	VI	VII	VIII	IX	X	XI	XII	I	II		III	IV	V	VI
Standard	0°	15°	30°	45°	60°	75°	90°	105°	120°		135°	150°	165°	180°
Chaddesley	0°	14°	26°	41°	54°	74°	90°	109°	126°	134°	140°	155°	169°	180°

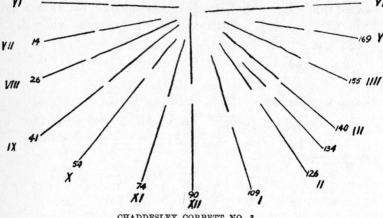

CHADDESLEY CORBETT NO. 3.

This dial is exceedingly interesting, because there can be no doubt as to what hours the lines are intended to mark, each line having a number attached to it.

It is not an accurately made dial, for the top lines are not horizontal, and most of the lines do not correspond with the Standard.

Thus the interval between	9 and 10 o'clock	= 13°
,,	,,	,,	10 ,, 11	,,	= 20°
,,	,,	,,	7 ,, 8	,,	= 12°
,,	,,	,,	2 ,, 3	,,	= 14°

This last interval is divided by an extra line, the only one having no number, and no doubt meant to represent 2.30, but the angle at which it is placed, 134°, corresponds almost exactly with 3 p.m. on the Standard Dial.

From these inaccuracies it is clear that dependence

was placed on the gnomon for the correct time, and the probability is this was first placed in the wall and the lines drawn as the shadows fell. This would be satisfactory for only one period of the year : for the rest the style would have to be altered, perhaps several times.

For illustration, see Plate XII; for description, see p. 189.

Downton. 17 inches in diameter. Aspect, due south.

The style-hole is square. The tracing with extended lines shows a most accurate dial. Six of the lines are 1° short, five are correct, and two are 1° over.

This affords a good example of the degree of accuracy shown by the method of tracing and line extension.

Hours	.	VI	VII	VIII	IX	X	XI	XII	I	II	III	IV	V	VI
Standard	.	0°	15°	30°	45°	60°	75°	90°	105°	120°	135°	150°	165°	180°
Downton	.	0°	15°	29°	44°	59°	74°	90°	104°	121°	136°	149°	165°	180°

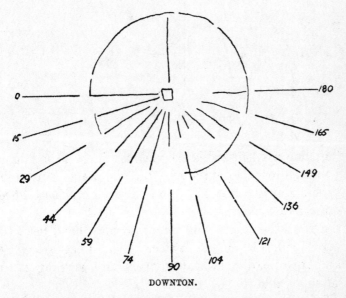

DOWNTON.

For illustration, see Plate V ; for description, see p. 187.

South Hayling No. 1.   Aspect, due south.

The workmanship of this dial is bad, and it is impossible to tell quite what the maker intended.   The lines are not straight and many do not point to the centre of the style-hole.

Hours	VI	VII	VIII	IX		X	XI	XII	I		II	III	IV	V	VI
Standard	0°	15°	30°	45°		60°	75°	90°	105°		120°	135°	150°	165°	180°
S. Hayling	0°		28°		51°		74°	90°		116°			155°	167°	180°

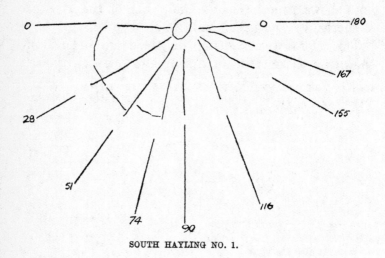

SOUTH HAYLING NO. 1.

The line marked 28° is the clearest line, and so might be meant for the Mass-line, but its angle certainly corresponds with line 155°, and so probably these lines mark 8 and 4 o'clock.

On the other hand, the intention may have been to mark 9, 10, 11 and 12 o'clock.   The lines are very plain, but so badly cut that any certainty with regard to it is impossible.

For illustration, see Plate IX ; for description, p. 154.

Herriard No. 1. Aspect, due south.

Hours	.	.	.	X	XI	XII
Standard	.	.	.	60°	75°	90°
Herriard	.	.	.	62°	76°	90°

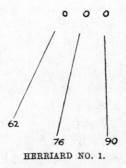

HERRIARD NO. 1.

The angles 62°, 76° and 90° are obviously intended for the hours 10, 11 and 12.

For illustration, see Plate VII ; for description, p. 156.

Herriard No. 2. Aspect, due south.

This dial consists of a well-marked style-hole, three well-marked lines, and two very indistinct lines.

Hours	.	VII	VIII	IX	X	XI	XII	I	II	III		IV	V	VI
Standard	.	15°	30°	45°	60°	75°	90°	105°	120°	135°		150°	165°	180°
Herriard	.		28°				90°		119°		141°	161°		

A fairly accurate dial, and probably other lines formerly present have now disappeared.

The three good lines mark 8, 12 and 3.30, and it may be noted that this last line, 141°, is 1½° from 119° (119 + 15 + 7½ = 141½).

The two faint lines are difficult to draw accurately, but are probably meant for 2 and 5 o'clock.

On a dial facing due south there is never a shadow at 7 a.m. and always a shadow at 8 a.m.   In the afternoon

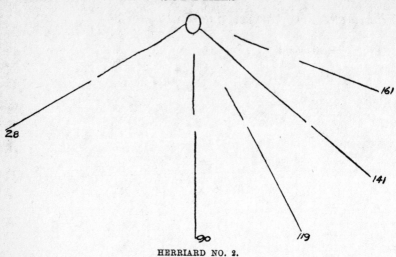

HERRIARD NO. 2.

there is never a shadow at 6 p.m., but at certain periods of the year there is a shadow at 5 p.m.[1]

For illustrations, see Plates VII and VIII; for description, p. 156.

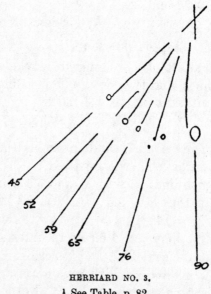

HERRIARD NO. 3.

[1] See Table, p. 82.

Herriard No. 3. Aspect, due south.

This dial consists of six lines, four of which extend to the style-hole, while the other two are short and indefinite. A very good dial.

Hours	IX		X		XI	XII
Standard.	45°		60°		75°	90°
Herriard.	45°	52°	59°	65°	76°	90°

Here we see the hours 9, 10, 11 and 12 accurately marked by the four long lines. The short lines no doubt are intended to mark 9.30 and 10.30.

For illustrations, see Plates VII and VIII ; for description, p. 156.

Herriard No. 4. Aspect, due south.

This dial has five lines, each ending in a hole. The left or western line is the most distinct, and passing to the right each line is less clearly cut, until the last or noon line is hardly visible.

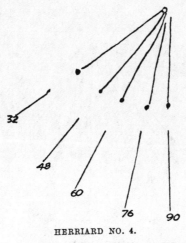

HERRIARD NO. 4.

Hours	.	VIII	IX	X	XI	XII
Standard	.	30°	45°	60°	75°	90°
Herriard	.	32°	48°	60°	76°	90°

In the tracing the most easterly line has been taken as vertical, but it probably bears a little to the east at its lower end ; it may be that the right-hand side of the shadow was intended to coincide with this line and not the centre of the shadow, as is usual. If this were so, it would throw all the other angles to the west and make the dial even more accurate.

It is quite evident that the lines were intended to mark 8, 9, 10, 11 and noon.

Note close to this dial, on the right (east), the remains of another dial, a style-hole, and parts of a complete circle.   No. 4A.

For illustrations, see Plates VII and VIII ; for description, p. 156.

Herriard No. 5.   Aspect, due south.

The lines on this dial are quite distinct except just around where the Mass-line might be expected to be found.   Perhaps the time of Mass varied, and the numer-

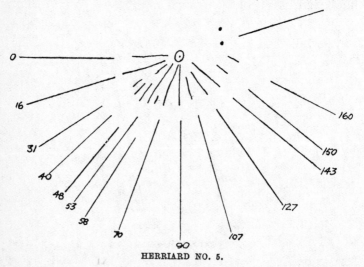

HERRIARD NO. 5.

ous lines here mark the various times, but the lines are so uncertain that the exact angles cannot be determined.

Hours	VI	VII	VIII		IX		X		XI	XII	I	II		III		IV	V
Standard .	0°	15°	30°		45°		60°		75°	90°	105°	120°		135°		150°	165°
Herriard .	0°	16°	31°	40°	48°	53° 58°		70°		90°	107°		127°		143°	1

Examining the lines round about 9 a.m. first, the line marked 53° is seen to be quite a good one. This may mark 9.30 ($45° + 7\frac{1}{2}° = 52\frac{1}{2}°$). The 48° line may be for 9 a.m. and the line 40° for 8.30 a.m.

A very indefinite line at 58° may be for 10 a.m.

The line 70°, if meant for 11 o'clock, is very inaccurate.

The 6, 7 and 8 o'clock lines are correctly placed, but on a dial like this facing due south there is never a shadow at 6 or 7 a.m.[1] The line 107° for 1 o'clock is fairly correct and 127° and 143° no doubt stand for 2.30 and 3.30 p.m.

There are two other lines, both very badly drawn, as neither passes through the style-hole, but they may represent 4 and 5 o'clock.

For illustration, see Plate VII ; for description, p. 157.

Herriard No. 6. Aspect, due south.

This dial, owing to the style-hole being blocked, the absence of many lines and its generally damaged condition, is impossible to trace and analyse with any degree of certainty.

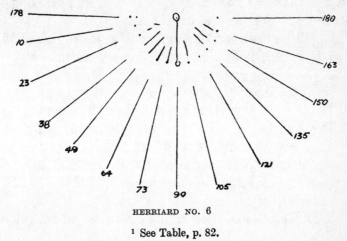

HERRIARD NO. 6

[1] See Table, p. 82.

An attempted tracing with extended lines shows :

Hours	VI	VII	VIII	IX	X	XI	XII	I	II	III	IV	V	VI
Standard	0°	15°	30°	45°	60°	75°	90°	105°	120°	135°	150°	165°	180°
Herriard	178°	10°	23°	38°	49°	64°	73°	90°	105°	121°	135°	150°	163°	180°

This is wonderfully accurate on the right-hand (east) side, every angle being almost absolutely correct.

The left-hand (west) side is not so good, but if the photo is examined it will be seen how difficult it is to be certain of the lines or holes. There are on this side seven lines instead of the usual six, and it may be that 10°, 23° and 38° are meant to represent 6.30, 7.30 and 8.30 a.m. The line 38°, it may be noted, is now the best-marked line on the dial.

For illustrations, see Plate VII ; for description, p. 157.

Laverstoke No. 1. This dial is now on the north wall and the doorway on which it is incised was probably situated on the south side of the church originally.

The description and tracing of the dial are included in this chapter in order to show that in its general construction it follows the usual plan.

It will be observed that the lines on it are placed 15° apart or some multiple of 15°, or some multiple of $7\frac{1}{2}$°, the latter being half 15°.

Thus the lines 36° and 66° are twice 15° apart.

The lines 36° and 111° are five times 15° apart.

The lines 66° and 111° are three times 15° apart.

Note also that the lines 90° and 111°, although not quite so accurately placed as the others, still are not very incorrect, for 90° + three times $7\frac{1}{2}$° ($22\frac{1}{2}$°) = $112\frac{1}{2}$°, an error of only $1\frac{1}{2}$°.

For illustration, see Plate X ; for description, p. 162.

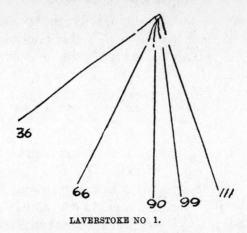

LAVERSTOKE NO 1.

St. Martin's, Salisbury.   Aspect, S. 20° E.

This dial has one line on the left (W.) above the horizontal. This may be presumed to be for 5 a.m. The dial faces S. 20° E., and my Experimental Dial No. VI, which faces S. 30° E., shows a shadow in June and July at 6 a.m., and it is possible that this dial might

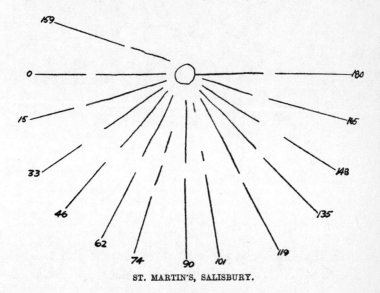

ST. MARTIN'S, SALISBURY.

show a shadow at 5 a.m., but if it did, the style would have to be bent *upwards*. A line in this position would be useless on a dial facing due south and even on one facing S. 15° E.

Hours	.	VI	VII	VIII	IX	X	XI	XII	I	II	III	IV	V	VI
Standard	.	0°	15°	30°	45°	60°	75°	90°	105°	120°	135°	150°	165°	180°
St. Martin's	.	0°	15°	33°	46°	62°	74°	90°	101°	119°	135°	148°	165°	180°

The lines are incised with a considerable degree of accuracy at equal distances of 15°. The only one showing much divergence is that marked 101°, which should be 105°, but if the photo is examined, it will be seen that it is really very difficult to see the true direction of this line.

For illustration, see Plate X ; for description, p. 188.

Martin No. 3.   Aspect, S. 36° E.

This dial is much overgrown with lichen.

Hours	VII	VIII	IX	X	XI	XII	I	II	III	IV	V	VI
Standard	15°	30°	45°	60°	75°	90°	105°	120°	135°	150°	167°	180°
Martin .	17°		44°		69°			120°	138°		165°	177°

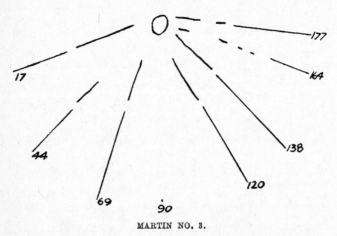

MARTIN NO. 3.

There seem to be three lines on the left and two on the right and two doubtful lines higher up. It is an irregular dial, inasmuch as the centre of the shadow does not seem to have been used ; but for the four lines to the left, the left-hand side, and in the three right upper lines the right side, of the shadow seem to have acted as the marker. The lines are seen drawn clearly to the left and the right of the style-hole, and not through its centre.

If the orientation is correct, it probably had a straight horizontal style, as there seems to be no vertical noon-line.

It can hardly be compared with my Experimental Dials Nos. VI and VII, as these mark the centre of the shadow.

On a dial like Experimental Dial No. VI, S. 30° E., there is seldom a shadow at 3 p.m., but on June 21 the following records appear :

Hours .	.	.	.	VI	VII	VIII	IX	X	II
Experimental Dial VI		.		18°	28°	42°		75°	125°
Martin	.	.	.	17°		44°		69°	120°

From these figures it would appear that this dial might have been used with a straight style as a fairly correct time-marker for the time round about midsummer,[1] but Dial No. VI has no shadow at this time after 2 p.m.

On a dial with an aspect like this, S. 36° E., there could never be a shadow at 4, 5 or 6 p.m.,[2] and yet there are two lines high up on the right-hand (east) side.

Perhaps this dial has been moved from some other position. It does not agree at all with Mr. Rosenberg's diagram for S. 35° E.

Martin No. 4.   Dial on Tower.   Aspect, S. 22° W.

A very interesting dial, having only three well-marked

---

[1] This is not a very probable explanation.
[2] See Table, p. 82.

lines, representing 10, 11 and 2 o'clock, the rest of the hours being marked by holes.

Hours	.	VII	VIII	IX	X	XI	XII	I	II	III	IV	V	VI	VII
Standard	.	15°	30°	45°	60°	75°	90°	105°	120°	135°	150°	165°	180°	15°
Martin	.	17°	29°	40°	58°	73°	90°	112°	126°	143°	155°	165°	4°	25°

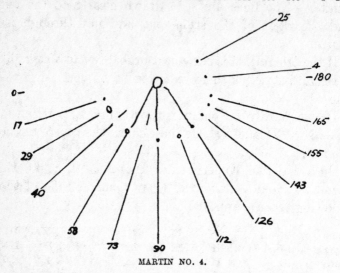

MARTIN NO. 4.

The dial is covered with lichen, and in consequence the holes are with difficulty seen. The angles, 15° apart, are fairly correct, especially on the left-hand (west) side.

Taking into account the aspect of this dial, it is obvious that if a shadow at noon was to fall on the line 90°, the gnomon must have been deflected to the east, as with a straight gnomon the shadow would always fall to the left (west) of the vertical line, for if the records of Experimental Dial No. IV [1] (which faces S. 15° W. and which has a straight gnomon) be referred to, it will be seen that noon is always marked on the west of the vertical line, at angles, at various times of the year, between 43° and 83°.

[1] P. 72.

There is no doubt that this dial would mark the
correct time if fitted with appropriate styles, deflected
to the east, and when necessary bent downwards.

But on a dial facing S. 22° W. there could never be a
shadow at 6 or 7 a.m.,[1] therefore the line marked 17°
would never be of use. One other feature of this dial
remains to be noticed, viz. the hole marked 25° on the
right-hand (east) side above the horizontal line.

It is interesting in this connection to compare this
dial (aspect, S. 22° *W*.) with the dial at St. Martin's,
Salisbury [2] (aspect, S. 20° *E*.). Both dials have a line or
hole above the horizontal lines, but this one at Martin
has a hole which marks an hour in the *evening*, the face
of the dial being turned towards the setting sun;
whereas at Salisbury the line marks an early hour in the
morning, the face of the dial being turned towards the
rising sun.

A horizontal style of course could not cast a shadow
upwards, but one bent upwards could, and so these two
dials furnish additional proof, if such be needed, in
favour of the " bent-style theory."

Martley.   No record of orientation.

Hours	VI	VII	VIII	IX	X	XI	XII	I	II	III	IV	V	VI
Standard	0°	15°	30°	45°	60°	75°	90°	105°	120°	135°	150°	165°	180°
Martley	19°	28°	39°	51°	64°	77°	90°	103°	118°	132°	146°	161°	177°

The spacing of the angles is much nearer the correct
on the right than on the left. The lines on this dial
extending higher on the right make it probable that it
faces somewhat to the west of south.

For illustration, see Plate X; for description, p. 192.

[1] See Table, p. 82.
[2] See *ante*, p. 125.

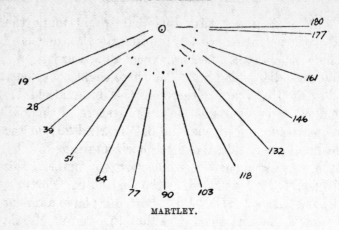

MARTLEY.

Penton Mewsey No. 1. Aspect, S. 20° W.

There is no incised horizontal line on this dial, but its place may be supposed to be taken by a masonry joint. If this is so, the vertical line does not form a right angle with it, but inclines to the west at its lower end.

Hours			X	XI	XII	I	II	III
Standard	.	.	60°	75°	90°	105°	120°	137°
Penton Mewsey	.	.	57°		90°	110°	121°	133°

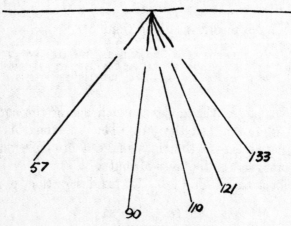

PENTON MEWSEY NO. 1.

There are three well-cut lines, and if the centre one is taken to mark 90°, then 10, 12 and 2 o'clock are correctly indicated. The two faint lines probably mark 1 and 3 o'clock. No doubt this dial had a style bent to the east, so that the shadow fell on the almost vertical line at noon.

For illustration, see Plate XI, and description, p. 166.

Sherborne St. John No. 1. Aspect, due south.

This is not a *very* accurate dial, and the vertical line inclines slightly to the east below. Possibly there is a horizontal line on each side, but they are too indefinite to trace.

Hours		*VIII*	IX	X	XI	*XII*	I	*II*	III	*IV*
Standard	.	30°	45°	60°	75°	90°	105°	120°	135°	150°
Sherborne	.	26°	49°	63°		90°		121°		152°

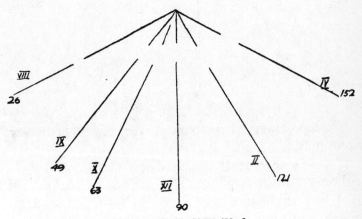

SHERBORNE ST. JOHN NO. 1.

No doubt the lines were intended to mark 8 and 4 and 10 and 2 o'clock, the 9 a.m. line being inserted for the time of Mass.

Looking at the dial without measurement it might be supposed that the very long line (26°) was the Mass-line and the next two lines were meant to mark 10 and 11 o'clock, but the protractor shows this not to be correct.

For illustration, see cover; for description, see p. 169.

Sherborne St. John No. 3. Aspect, due south.

A very small dial and high up on the wall.

Hours	.	VI	VII	VIII	IX	X	XI	XII	I	II	III	IV	V	VI
Standard	.	0°	15°	30°	45°	60°	75°	90°	105°	120°	135°	150°	165°	180°
Sherborne	.	0°		28°		58°		90°		120°		151°		180°

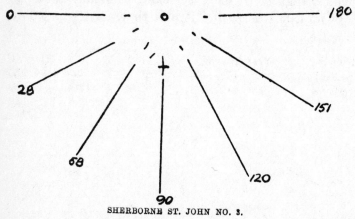

SHERBORNE ST. JOHN NO. 3.

The lines are seen here to mark every second hour very accurately.

Note the cross on the vertical line.

For illustration, see Plate XV; for description, p. 170.

A further illustration of a dial at Sherborne St. John appears on Plate VI.

Steventon No. 2. Aspect, S. 12° W.

This remarkable, but extremely interesting, dial has been slightly damaged on the right-hand side, but the lines are placed with wonderful accuracy.

Hours		VI	VII	7.30	VIII	IX	X	10.30	XI	XII	I	1.30	II	III	IV	4.30	V	VI
Standard		0°	15°		30°	45°	60°		75°	90°	105°		120°	135°	150°		165°	180°
Steventon	Deeply cut lines (– – –)	0°				46°				90°				137°				180°
	Other lines (– . – .)		23°				68°								160°			
	3rd set of lines (——)				30°	58°			77°		102°						170°	

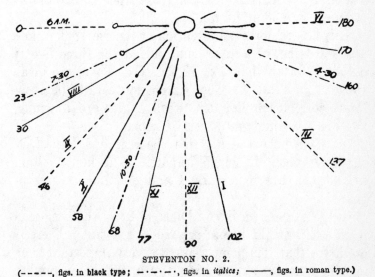

STEVENTON NO. 2.

(– – – –, figs. in **black type**; – . – . – ., figs. in *italics*; ——, figs. in roman type.)

It will be observed that certain of the lines are much more deeply cut than others, and end in well-marked holes. These well-marked lines divide the half-circle into eight equal parts. This conveys the impression of an old Saxon dial with each division halved. The right-hand side (E.) does not show this quite so well as the left, as a part of this side has been damaged and the noon-line is not particularly well-cut.

Apart from these deficiencies, one can plainly see a 6 a.m. and 6 p.m. line and a noon-line halving the half-circle, then each quadrant is divided in half by another line (9 and 3 o'clock), producing four equal divisions, and so being exactly like a Saxon dial. Beyond this each of these divisions is again halved, and so eight equal divisions are formed.

Three of these last divisions are again halved, but the lines marking these halvings are not so deeply cut and do not end in holes. The eight primary divisions undoubtedly mark 6, 7.30, 9, 10.30 a.m., 12 noon (1.30 missing), 3, 4.30 and 6 p.m.

This was the original intention of the dial maker, and afterwards he, or a later hand, added the three lightly cut lines for the hours 8, 10 and 11. There are in all thirteen lines, and of these six may be said to be absolutely correct, one line is 1° wrong, three are 2° wrong, two are 3° wrong, and one is 5° wrong.

On the whole, the dial may be regarded as perfect, the lines being 15° or 7½° apart. The hours 7 a.m. and 4 p.m. are not marked and 2 p.m. has disappeared.

In the chapter on Saxon Dials, p. 22 f., the Dæg-mæl point was brought before the reader's notice. There is no doubt that this point marked a very important time in the Saxonic period, viz. 7.30 a.m., the beginning of the first tide of the day, and accordingly we sometimes find it specially stressed by having a cross or a swastika incised on the line marking this time. The Steventon dial has a distinct bearing on this point, and so reference is again made to it.

When the writer began to analyse dials by measuring the exact angles formed by the lines on them, he was much surprised to find that in a number of instances the half-hours were marked. The first hasty conclusion he came to was that these half-hour markings simply showed a want of accuracy on the part of the dial-maker. On further consideration this explanation was found to be wrong, and here again

Haigh's classical paper on Yorkshire dials proved very helpful.[1]

No doubt the Norman conquerors were able to impose the twelve-hour day on the beaten Anglo-Saxons and the duodecimal system became the official system of time reckoning ; but when we consider our own summer-time regulations and the opposition they provoked, we may readily suppose the country folk, at least among the Saxons, clung to their old method. At 7.30 a.m. they were accustomed to breakfast ; indeed, it was the time of the first principal meal of the day, and so they were not likely easily to fall into the new method, which did not make any serious attempt to mark this time. And so also the midday period and the Ofanvertha dagr (the day passing over, from $1\frac{1}{2}$ to $4\frac{1}{2}$ p.m.), and the mid-afternoon from $4\frac{1}{2}$ to $7\frac{1}{2}$ p.m. would not be speedily forgotten.

Bearing in mind these circumstances, the fact that lines are sometimes found on Mass-clocks half-way between the hour-lines is not very surprising. It would seem as if the makers of them sometimes compromised matters, and while adhering to the old method in part, they also fell in with the new method to a still greater extent.

Looked at from this standpoint, the Steventon dial is very instructive. All the hours belonging to the duodecimal system except 7 a.m. and 4 p.m. are marked on this dial, and in addition 7.30, 10.30 a.m. (1.30 p.m. destroyed) and 4.30 p.m., these times marking the commencements of the four important tides of the day.

I do not know if there are many dials now extant which exhibit this compromise between the new and the old systems, but besides this Steventon dial, in which it is plainly evident, traces of it can be seen in the following

[1] See p. 22 f.

dials, viz. Bramley No. 5 (p. 110), Burghclere No. 4
(p. 112), Herriard No. 6 (p. 123), Stoke Charity No. 6
(p. 138), Up Nateley (p. 139) and Warnford No. 1
(p. 140).

In a former chapter the difficulty of dating Mass-
clocks has been pointed out, and in this connexion it
would be reasonable to suppose that dials showing this
peculiar blending of Saxon and Norman methods
would be, in point of time, those made soon after
the Conquest [1] and before the new system had entirely
ousted the old one, and so, on further investigation in
various parts of the country, it may be found that dials
of this variety may prove to have some chronological
significance.

For illustration, see Plate XIII; for description,
p. 172.

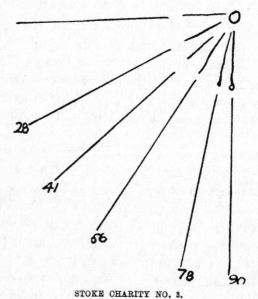

STOKE CHARITY NO. 3.

[1] This does not necessarily mean a few years, for the Steventon dial
could not be earlier than c. 1200.

Stoke Charity No. 3.   Aspect, due south.

Here the angles are not very accurately drawn, but sufficiently so to show that 15° apart was the intention of the maker.

Hours .	.	VI	VII	VIII	IX	X	XI	XII
Standard	.	0°	15°	30°	45°	60°	75°	90°
Stoke Charity .		0°		28°	41°	56°	78°	90°

The dial faces due south, and with that aspect would never have a shadow at either 6 or 7 a.m.[1] It does not fit in with Mr. Rosenberg's theory.

For illustration, see Plate XIII; for description, p. 174.

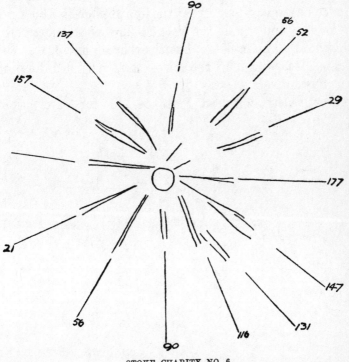

STOKE CHARITY NO. 6.

[1] See Table, p. 82.

Stoke Charity No. 6.   Aspect, due south.

A tracing of an enlarged photograph shows in the lower half :

Hours		VI	VIII	X	XII	II	IV	VI
Standard	.	0°	30°	60°	90°	120°	150°	180°
Stoke Charity	.		21°	56°	90°	116°	147°	177°

The intention here is evidently to have a dial with lines at two-hourly intervals, and the angles are all fairly correct except for the line marking 8 a.m. ; but in reference to this line it may be pointed out that it is 32° from the line above it, which is intended for the horizontal line, but slopes upwards at its western end. It seems more probable that the line 21° marks 7.30 a.m.[1]

In the upper half the vertical line is so incorrectly drawn as to be useless ; but the scheme here shows the same idea as that in the lower half, viz. lines dividing the day into six parts.

For illustration, see Plate XIII ; for description, p. 175.

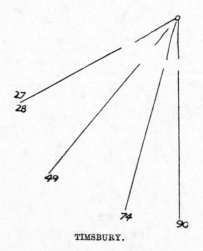

27
28

49

74   90

TIMSBURY.

[1] See p. 134 f., under Steventon.

Timsbury.   Aspect, due south.

The apparently vertical line possibly slopes to the east.

Hours	.	.	VI	VII	VIII	IX	X	XI	XII
Standard	.		0°	15°	30°	45°	60°	75°	90°
Timsbury	.				28°	49°		74°	90°

The dial is covered with lichen and perhaps there are other lines.

For illustration, see Plate XIV; for description, p. 175.

Up Nateley.   Dial not *in situ.*   Aspect, now, S. 32° E.

Hours	.	VI	VII	VIII	IX	X	XI	XII	I	II	III
Standard	.	0°	15°	30°	45°	60°	75°	90°	105°	120°	135°
Up Nateley			20°	32°	49°	60°	77°	90°	105°	124°	136°

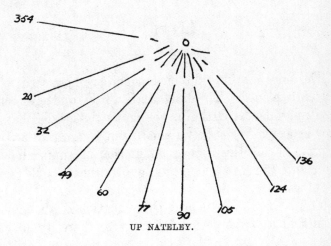

UP NATELEY.

Some reference has been made to this dial in Chapter IV, p. 52, and all that need be added here is that the lines are 15° apart, and that if fitted with a style facing due south, and when necessary bent down at various angles, it would tell the time at every season of the year with a very fair degree of accuracy.

For illustration, see Plate XIV ; for description, p. 176.

Warnford No. 1.　　Aspect, S. 15° E.

Hours	.	VI	VII	7.30	VIII	IX	X	XI	XII	V
Standard	.	0°	15°		30°	45°	60°	75°	90°	165°
Warnford	.			22°	31°	44°	60°	77°	90°	161°

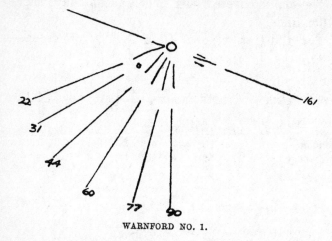

WARNFORD NO. 1.

The lines marking 8 a.m. to noon are here seen to be correctly placed. The dial faces S. 15° E., and a reference to Experimental Dial No. V [1] shows that a dial having this aspect never shows a shadow at 6 a.m. nor at 5 or 6 p.m. From this it is apparent that the upper line on each side (both of which are doubtful lines) could never be of any use.

From the Experimental Dial mentioned above it is seen that at some periods of the year there would be a shadow at 7 a.m.

Half-past 7 o'clock is probably the earliest time when a shadow might always be expected, and the line marked 22° is exactly 7.30 a.m. Nine in the morning is generally

[1] See Table, p. 82.

PLATE I

BARFRESTON, Nos. 4, 5 & 6
Description p. 185. *Analysis p.* 105.

BARFRESTON, Nos. 7 & 8
Description p. 186. *Analysis p.* 107.

BARFRESTON, Nos. 1, 2 & 3
Description p. 184. *Analysis p.* 104.

BINSTEAD
Description p. 181.

PLATE II

BREAMORE No. 1
Description p. 145.

BREAMORE No. 2
Description p. 145.

BAUGHURST No. 2
Description p. 143.

BURGHCLERE Nos. 4 & 5
Description p. 147.   *Analysis p.* 112.

PLATE III

BURGHCLERE Nos. 6 & 7
Description p. 147.

BURGHCLERE 1, 2 & 3
Description p. 146. *Analysis p.* 111.

NORTH CERNEY No. 1
Description p. 183.

CHERITON
Description p. 149.

PLATE IV

BEAMLEY No. 5

Description p. 145.   *Analysis p.* 110.

BRAMLEY Nos. 3 & 4

Description p. 144.   *Analysis p.* 109.

HOLT

Description p. 191.

CHADDERSLEY No. 2

Description p. 189.   *Analysis p.* 115.

PLATE V

CORHAMPTON, SAXON DIAL
Description p. 19.

CHALTON
Description p. 148.

SOUTH DAMERHAM No. 1
Description p. 150.

DOWNTON
Description p. 187. *Analysis p.* 117.

PLATE VI

CHILCOMB
Description p. 149.

FORDINGBRIDGE
Description p. 152.

SHERBORNE ST. JOHN No. 5
Description p. 171.

SHERBORNE ST. JOHN No. 2
Description p. 169.

PLATE VII

HERRIARD Nos. 5, 6 & 7
Descriptions p. 157.   *Analysis pp.* 122, 123.

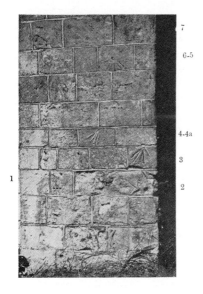

HERRIARD
THE WHOLE BUTTRESS
Dials 1, 2, 3, 4, 4A, 5, 6 & 7
Description pp. 155—157.

HERRIARD No. 1
Description p. 156.   *Analysis p.* 119.

PLATE VIII

HERRIARD Nos. 2, 3, 4 & 4A
Descriptions pp. 156, 157. *Analyses pp.* 119—121.

HURSTBORNE PRIORS
Description p. 159.

HOUGHTON
Description p. 158.

PLATE IX

BISHOP'S SUTTON No. 3

DIAL NO. 3 AND A 'BROAD ARROW'

Descriptions pp. 143 *&* 43. *Analysis p.* 108.

SOUTH HAYLING No. 1

Description p. 154. *Analysis p.* 118.

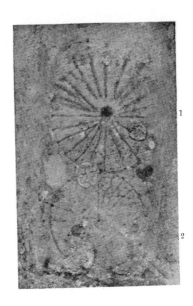

IDSWORTH Nos. 1 & 2

Description p. 159.

KING'S SOMBORNE Nos. 1 & 2

Description p. 162.

PLATE X

LAVERSTROKE No. 1
Description p. 162. *Analysis p.* 124.

MARTIN Nos. 1 & 2
Description p. 163.

MARTLEY
Description p. 192. *Analysis p.* 129.

ST. MARTIN'S, SALISBURY
Description p. 188. *Analysis p.* 125.

PLATE XI

PENTON MEWSEY No. 1
Description p. 166. *Analysis p.* 130.

PRESTON CONDOVER
Description p. 166.

ROWNER Nos. 1 & 2
Description p. 168.

STOULTON No. 1
Description p. 192.

PLATE XII

SHALFLEET
Description p. 182.

BAUGHURST No. 1
Description p. 142.

CHADDERSLEY CORBETT No. 3
Description p. 189. Analysis p. 116.

CALBORNE. ISLE OF WIGHT. DIALS 1 & 2
Description p. 181.

PLATE XIII

2

3

4

STOKE CHARITY No. 6
Description p. 175. Analysis p. 138.

STOKE CHARITY Nos. 2, 3 & 4
Description p. 174. Analysis p. 137.

STEVENTON No. 2
Description p. 172. Analysis p. 132.

STEVENTON No. 3
Description p. 172.

PLATE XIV

TIMSBURY

Description p. 175. *Analysis p.* 139.

UPHAM

Description p. 176.

UP NATELEY

Description p. 176. *Analysis p.* 139.

WARNFORD No. 1 & 2

Description p. 178. *Analysis p.* 140.

PLATE XV

YAVERLAND
Description p. 183.

WONSTON No. 3
Description p. 180.

1

2

WINCHFIELD Nos. 1 & 2
Description p. 179.

SHERBORNE ST. JOHN No. 3
Description p. 170. *Analysis p.* 132.

PLATE XVI

THE AUTHOR'S EXPERIMENTAL DIALS
Description pp. 46—48.

supposed to have been the usual time for Mass in the pre-Reformation Church, and this dial has 9 a.m. marked by an exceedingly well-cut line at 44°.

Why 8 a.m. should be marked by a hole and no line it is impossible to tell; but with the exception of the doubtful upper lines, this dial may be considered a good example of accurate workmanship.

For illustration, see Plate XIV; for description, p. 178.

CHAPTER X

CATALOGUE RAISONNÉ

THE dials are described here under their respective counties and are arranged alphabetically.

HAMPSHIRE

ASHE. Visited July 14, 1924. One dial.

Very little is left of this dial. It is at the east end of the sill of the middle window on the *north* side of the nave. This church was built in 1877 on an old site and a few details of the old church are preserved.

BAUGHURST. Visited July 16, 1924. Two dials.

This is a modern church, but a late twelfth-century doorway, blocked, has been inserted in the west wall of the nave. It is on this doorway that these two dials are situated, and it is to be noted that both appear to be *inverted*.

1. Dial on north jamb of west doorway. There is no style-hole: it must have been in the masonry joint. There are five lines all radiating upwards and all ending in small holes. One of these lines is vertical and there are two on each side of it. The style-hole was about 30 inches from the ground and the lines 3½ inches long. No circle. It is to be noted that, as the stone on which this dial is cut has part of an attached shaft carved on it, if, when the doorway was reused, the stone was turned upside-down, it must also have been moved from one side of the doorway to the opposite jamb. It faces *west* now. (Photo, Plate XII.)

2. This dial is on the south jamb of the *west* doorway

and is also inverted. The style-hole is about 26 inches from the ground and is surrounded by two perfect circles and in the upper part by a portion of another outer circle. There are seven lines, none of which starts from the style-hole, and five of them seem only to extend between the two inner circles. One line extends from the inner to the outer circle, and the vertical line is prolonged beyond the outer circle and ends in a cross. No holes. It faces *west* now. (Photo, Plate II.)

BISHOP'S SUTTON. Visited September 12, 1923. Three dials.

1. This dial is on the west outer jamb of the south doorway, now covered by a modern porch. The doorway is of Norman origin, *c.* 1150, and is ornamented with beak-heads. The dial has a style-hole in a masonry joint 63 inches from the ground and on the west a part of a circle. There are four lines radiating downwards which measure $3\frac{1}{2}$ inches. It faces due south.

2. On the south doorway is another dial, very indistinct. It is on the *inner* jamb. The style-hole is in stone and there are four lines radiating downwards. Style-hole from ground $57\frac{1}{2}$ inches. Radii $3\frac{1}{2}$ inches. Faces due south.

3. This dial, a very clear one, is on one of the original large quoins, *c.* 1150, at the south-east corner of the nave. It faces S. 2° W. (Plate IX.)

The style-hole is in a joint, and below this is an irregular half-circle with radii about 4 inches long. The style-hole is 52 inches from the ground. This is a most interesting dial, possibly used in the summer only, and it has thirteen lines, including those formed by the masonry joint, but no line is truly vertical. (See Analysis, p. 108. Photo, Plate IX.)

Below the last dial, and on a similar quoin, is a mark

which the Victoria County History calls another dial.
This is not a dial, but undoubtedly an Ordnance Survey
bench-mark. A description of these "broad arrow"
marks will be found on p. 43.

BRAMLEY. Visited July 16, 1924. Five dials.

This most interesting church retains part of the rood-
screen and the ceiling over the rood, but its greatest
treasure is a thirteenth-century wall-painting of the
martyrdom of St. Thomas of Canterbury, and here also
is a large fifteenth-century one of St. Christopher, both
recently judiciously restored.

There are five dials here, all on the south doorway of
the chancel. This doorway has a continuous chamfer and
a pointed head, and the Victoria County History dates
it *c.* 1360. These dials, therefore, it would seem, cannot
be earlier than that date. They all face due south.

1. Dial on west jamb of south chancel doorway. The
style-hole, blocked, is about 36 inches from the ground.
The west side of the dial is covered over with cement,
otherwise there is a complete circle with a diameter of
7 inches. The stone has been re-tooled and only three
lines are visible.

2. A dial about 12 inches above No. 1. This small
dial, 2 inches in diameter, has a complete circle and eight
lines dividing it into eight equal portions.

3. Dial on east jamb of south chancel doorway. The
lowest of three dials. The style-hole, large and damaged,
is about 32 inches from the ground. A circle can be
seen in the upper half or more, and in the lower part are
seven lines, badly cut, all radiating downwards. (See
Analysis, p. 109. Photo, Plate IV.)

4. On the stone above No. 3. An imperfect dial with
style-hole and in the lower half six lines. (Photo,
Plate IV.)

5. Dial on east jamb of south chancel doorway. The highest of three dials. The style-hole is blocked and is about 50 inches from the ground. Probably there was a complete circle, 6 inches in diameter. Thirteen or fourteen lines can be seen, two in the south-east quadrant being well-marked, and many of the lines end in small holes. On the western side of this dial many of the lines are filled with cement. (See Analysis, p. 110. Photo, Plate IV.)

BREAMORE. Visited July 9, 1923. Three dials.

This interesting, and very little altered, pre-Conquest church has three dials.

1. This dial is on a quoin at the west angle of the south porch, which seems to have been added in the middle of the twelfth century. It faces S. 1° E.

The dial, which is contained in a circle 2 inches in diameter, has thirteen holes remaining round the circumference and a style-hole 60 inches from the ground. Seven or eight lines are visible, which, starting in holes at the circumference, are generally not continued to the style-hole. A very small dial. (Photo, Plate II.)

The other two dials are on quoins at the south-east angle of the south transept. The stone is much worn, and faces S. 1° E. The south transept is part of the unaltered pre-Conquest church, and the quoins at the angles show massive long and short work.

2. The upper dial has a large style-hole, 76 inches from the ground, and perhaps had a circle. In the eastern half there are four lines, the upper one slanting upwards, and in the western half one line. The only two really distinct lines are the lowest one on each side, of which one, the eastern, measures 5 inches. (Photo, Plate II.)

3. The lower dial is on the quoin next below. The only traces left of it are the style-hole and two lines.

BROCKENHURST. Visited June 10, 1924. One dial
    with remains of style.

The dial here is on the east jamb of the south porch
doorway. It faces S. 22° W. The arch of the doorway is
built of a red stone and is of one pointed order, with
a chamfer continued down to the ground and of late
thirteenth-century date.

Only about half of the dial can now be seen, the rest
being covered with plaster, with which the porch has
been covered. The visible part is the western half,
which is contained in an indistinct circle. In the upper
part of the dial one line can be seen ending in a hole, and
in the lower part there is a horizontal line to the west
and a vertical line, and between these there are four lines
and some holes. These latter lines do not extend to the
circle, which has a radius of 2 inches. It is but very
rarely that a dial is found with its style *in situ*, but this
dial retains its metal style (? iron), broken off and
projecting about $\frac{1}{16}$th of an inch. The diameter of this
projecting piece of metal appears to be rather less than
$\frac{1}{8}$th of an inch ; and this is interesting because so little
is known of the size of the style in all these dials, and if
they fitted the style-holes which are so frequently seen
they must have been much thicker than this one.

BURGHCLERE. Visited July 17, 1924. Seven dials.

Five of the dials found here are on the south doorway
of the nave, which is of twelfth-century date and is
blocked.

Three dials are on the east jamb. They all face due
south. (Photo, Plate III.)

1. Dial on sixth stone from ground. The style-hole
is 57 inches from the ground, and there are four or five
lines ; the upper two or three are cut short by the
chamfered edge of the jamb. All the lines are in the

lower western quadrant, and the longest is 4 inches in length. Part of a circle is seen in the lowest portion.

2. Dial on fifth stone up. The style-hole is 47 inches from the ground. A very imperfect dial, only one line being clear, but there are traces of others. Radius $3\frac{1}{2}$ inches. Vertically below the style-hole there is a small hole. (See Analysis, p. 111.)

3. Dial on fourth stone up. The style-hole is 36 inches from the ground. A fairly good dial but covered with lichen, and six lines all radiating downwards, can be seen, the longest being 5 inches in length.

Two dials are on the west jamb. They face due south. (Plate II.)

4. The upper dial has a style-hole $46\frac{1}{2}$ inches from the ground, and there is a complete circle $3\frac{1}{2}$ inches in diameter. Twelve lines can be seen plainly, mostly in the lower half. No holes. (See Analysis, p. 112.)

5. The lower dial, on the same stone, which is covered with lichen.

It consists of a style-hole $43\frac{1}{2}$ inches from the ground, and vertically below it a hole. To the west of the style-hole is a horizontal line, which, however, seems to slope somewhat upwards. Between this line and the vertical hole is another line which has a hole at its extremity. (See Analysis, p. 113.)

Two dials are on the south-east angle of the Nave. They face S. 8° E. (Photo, Plate III.)

This wall dates from 1100 to 1120.

6. This dial, much obscured by lichen, has a style-hole 60 inches from the ground and a complete circle $5\frac{1}{2}$ inches in diameter. No lines or holes can be seen.

7. This dial is also covered with lichen. The style-hole, 2 inches deep, is 52 inches from the ground. There is a complete circle 5 inches in diameter.

Twelve lines, all in the lower half, can be seen, some ending in holes, and there is a quite distinct hole in the upper half of the circle dividing it into two equal parts. This dial, when analysed, proves to be extraordinarily interesting.　(See Analysis, p. 114.)

CATHERINGTON.　Visited June 16, 1925.　One dial.

This dial is on the east jamb of the south doorway of the south aisle.　The doorway, which has a semicircular head and nook-shafts with foliate capitals, probably dates from *c*. 1190.

The dial, which is a very indistinct one, faces due south.　The style-hole, the only part easily seen now, is 56 inches from the ground.　A vertical line can be distinguished and traces of some others, but the stone is broken away on the right (east) and much weathered all over.

CHALTON.　Visited June 16, 1925.　One dial.

The dial here is incised on the east side of the arch of the pointed priests' doorway, now blocked, on the south of the chancel.　The arch belongs to work executed in the middle of the thirteenth century, but the jambs are modern.　The dial is contained in a double circle, the diameter of the outer one measuring $4\frac{1}{2}$ inches. The style-hole is in a mortar-joint and is 67 inches from the ground.　Six lines can be seen, all in the lower half, three being in the left (west) quadrant and three in the right (east) quadrant.　No vertical line can be seen. The aspect is S. 15° E.

Special interest is attached to this dial because it is cut on two stones which form part of a thirteenth-century arch, the joint between the two stones dividing the dial into two equal parts and containing the style-hole.

It is from a consideration of these facts that a clue

may be obtained as to the date of the dial, for quite obviously it cannot have been moved from a Norman doorway and must be assigned to a date not earlier than about 1250. (See photo of arch and dial, Plate V.)

CHERITON. Visited July 1922. One dial.

This dial is on the top stone, immediately under the capital of the east jamb of the doorway of the south porch. This is a thirteenth-century structure, and is built of two kinds of stone, the one probably from Binstead and the other a soft yellow stone, and it is on a piece of the latter that the dial is incised. The right-hand lower corner of the stone is not present. The dial faces due south, and, although plainly visible, the workmanship is bad.

There are thirteen lines in the lower half, including a horizontal one on each side, and in the upper half one short line radiating upwards and to the east. The line next to the vertical one on the west is straight, deep, and well-cut. The style-hole seems to have been large, but is filled with plaster; it is $57\frac{1}{2}$ inches from the ground. The vertical line is $2\frac{1}{2}$ inches long. No circle. (Good photo, Plate III.)

CHILCOMBE. Visited July 1922. One dial.

The church dates from c. 1130 to 1140, and the dial is high up on a quoin of Binstead stone at the south-east angle of the nave. It faces due south. The style-hole is 82 inches from the ground, but repairs to the roof being in progress, a photograph was taken by standing on a ladder and some scaffolding. In this photo there is the shadow cast by a scaffolding pole on the east side of the dial.

The lines of the dial, ten in number, are generally clearly cut, and consist of a vertical one with five on the western and four on the eastern side. The vertical line is 5 inches and the side lines 6 inches long. There is no circle and all the lines radiate downwards.

The very numerous holes seen in the photo are such as are usually found in weathered Binstead stone. (Photo, Plate VI.)

SOUTH DAMERHAM. Visited July 20, 1923. Three dials.

1. There is a rather large, good dial on the east jamb of the doorway of the south porch, which was built in the latter part of the fifteenth century. It faces S. 5° E., and twenty lines, or parts of lines, remain visible, some ending in holes. The style-hole, which is large, is 53½ inches from the ground, and the dial measures 9½ inches in diameter.

It seems reasonable to suppose this was originally a full-wheel dial with twenty-four lines, the four missing lines being absent from the western upper quadrant, but one at least of these is marked by a distinct hole. (Photo, Plate V.)

2. There are two dials on a buttress which projects to the south at the south-west angle of the nave. Both face S. 12° E.

The upper and largest dial had its style-hole in a masonry joint 38 inches from the ground. There are thirteen lines in the lower half, if the two horizontal lines formed by the joint be included, thus forming a half-wheel dial. The vertical line is 4 inches long and the lines on the west are about the same length, but the eastern lines are much longer, some of them measuring 7½ inches, and on this side there are numerous small holes.

3. The lower dial, cut on the stone next below, has a style-hole 38 inches from the ground and only three lines,

all of which are in the lower western quadrant. They are 6 inches long.

DROXFORD. Visited February 18, 1925. Four dials.

1. A dial on the east jamb of the south Norman doorway (1150–1160). This doorway has been twice moved, firstly in the first half of the thirteenth century, and secondly in the latter part of the fifteenth or early in the sixteenth century. There is no style-hole to be seen now. A complete circle is present with four short lines at the circumference in the lower part. Portions of the dial and of the lines are much broken.

From the centre of the circle to the ground is 53 inches. Diameter 6 inches. The dial may not be *in situ*, but it now faces due south.

2. A dial on west jamb of the same doorway (see above). Style-hole blocked, 51 inches from the ground. An indistinct circle is seen in the lower half with three lines which are 2 inches long. One line is drawn from the style-hole vertically downwards, and the other two are in the lower western quadrant.

3. There are two dials on the stones forming the east jamb of the east window of the fourteenth-century south-east chapel. This chapel dates from *c.* 1300.

A large dial, about 10 feet from the ground. It consists of a complete circle having a diameter of about 11 inches. There are two horizontal lines, and in the lower half five lines, some ending in holes, and there are some holes without visible lines. Faces S. 2° W. A good dial.

4. A very large dial, two stones below No. 3. It consists of a circle and four lines : the latter, which are not accurately cut, divide the circle into four quadrants. The circle extends on to the stone below, which forms the sill of the window. Diameter, 12½ inches. Style-hole 71½ inches from the ground.

ELLINGHAM. Visited August 21, 1922. One dial.

This church will well repay a visit. In the churchyard is the grave of Dame Alicia Lisle, aged 70, tried by Jefferies at the Bloody Assize and beheaded in Winchester market-place, 1685, probably the last woman so to suffer. Among many interesting things in the church the most uncommon is the plastered tympanum over the chancel screen and part of rood-loft, of date c. 1460.

A very large painted sundial, dated 1720, fills the gable of the porch.

On the south face of the south-east buttress of the chancel is a dial, a half-circle 10½ inches in diameter, with a style-hole 71½ inches from the ground. It faces S. 10° E. The church is a late thirteenth-century structure, and the buttress is probably contemporary. The dial is not very plain, but there is an inner half-circle with some holes on it, and most of the lines do not extend beyond this. Of the lines, the vertical and two horizontal lines all extend to the outer circle, and there are three other shorter lines on each side of the vertical one.

FORDINGBRIDGE. Visited August 21, 1923. One dial.

This dial is on the south face of the eastern of two angular buttresses at the south-east corner of the chancel. These are early thirteenth-century buttresses. It is one of those dials where all the lines occupy what would be the lower and western quadrant of a circle. The style-hole, 70 inches from the ground, is in a masonry joint, which joint may be considered to form a horizontal line. There is a vertical line and to the west of it five other lines, but between the highest of these and the horizontal joint there is a considerable gap. The radii measure 5 inches. It faces S. 30° E. The photo had to be taken hurriedly. because a shadow was rapidly advancing over the dial. The other angular buttress projects to the south to such an extent as to cause this dial to be in the shade in the afternoon, and this accounts for the absence of lines in the eastern quadrant. (Photo, Plate VI.)

There are also here two holes which appear to be style-holes on a buttress on the south of the nave, east of the porch. This is a fifteenth-century buttress.

HAMBLEDON. Visited February 18, 1925. One dial.

This is on the east jamb of the priest's doorway. The style-hole is plainly seen, but nothing else beyond a very indistinct circle is visible.

NORTH HAYLING. Visited June 27, 1924. Two dials.

1. This church has a dial in a most unusual situation, being on the slanting face of the set-off of a buttress; the surface of the dial faces therefore in an upward direction. The buttress is on the south-east corner of the chancel. The set-off consists of one block of stone, the slanting face of which is covered with lichen, and has two crosses incised on it and the dial, the latter being placed in the left-hand half. The bottom of the set-off is 3 feet 6 inches from the ground. The dial, which is enclosed in a circle, is $3\frac{3}{4}$ inches in diameter. The style-hole is 1 inch deep, and is closed by a chunk of mortar, and the lines which radiate from it in all directions are not very easily seen, but perhaps are about ten in number.

2. There is also a dial on the east jamb of the priest's doorway at the south-west of the chancel. This faces S. 2° W. The style-hole is 50 inches from the ground and the lines measure $2\frac{3}{8}$ inches. The dial, which consists of the lower half of a circle, has ten lines, two or three of which are prolonged beyond the circle. There are a vertical line and two horizontal ones, and in the western quadrant there are three lines and in the

eastern quadrant four lines. The next line to the west of the vertical line ends outside the circle in a hole.

The chancel of this church belongs to the thirteenth century.

The writer wishes to acknowledge the great assistance he has received in respect to the dials on this church from Mr. E. S. McEuan, of Richmond House, Hayling Island.

SOUTH HAYLING. Visited June 27, 1924. Four dials.

This church is a mid-thirteenth century structure, the chancel being the earliest part.

1. This dial is on a quoin at the south-east corner of the south aisle. The stone is much weathered and faces due south. The style-hole is 2 feet $10\frac{3}{4}$ inches from the ground. Parts of a badly cut circle can be seen, and there are nine lines, one vertical and two horizontal, and in the west quadrant three lines and in the east quadrant three lines. The dial measures from east to west about $5\frac{1}{2}$ inches and the lines vary in length from 3 to 4 inches. (See Analysis, p. 118.) Photo sent me by Mr. E. S. McEuan. (Plate IX.)

2. This dial is on the wall at the west end of the chancel in the angle formed by the south aisle meeting the chancel, and on account of the projection of the former the dial could not have been of use after 12 o'clock. It faces S. 12° W. The style-hole is 3 feet 8 inches from the ground. There is a horizontal line to the west and a vertical line, and between these there are four lines.

3. There are some slight traces of another dial on the east jamb of the priest's door on the south of the chancel.

4. There is almost certainly a hole-dial on the south buttress (one of two clasping buttresses) at the south-east corner of the chancel and possibly the style-hole of another. The style-hole is 70 inches from the ground,

and there are four holes all in the lower half at distances of from $2\frac{1}{2}$ to $3\frac{1}{4}$ inches.

I am much indebted to Mr. E. S. McEuan, of Richmond House, Hayling Island, for his generous help with regard to the dials on this church and also for the excellent photo.

HEADBOURNE WORTHY. Visited March 24, 1922. One dial.

This interesting church, with its remains of pre-Conquest work, including a very large dignified stone rood, has a dial on the tower, which is situated at the south-west angle of the nave and was added in the thirteenth century.

The dial is on the south face of a quoin, about 10 feet from the ground, which forms part of the south-east angle of the tower. The walls of the tower are of flint, but the angle-quoins are of Binstead stone. The dial is small and very indistinct, except that the style-hole is well marked and rather large. One can imagine the outline of a circle, but the whole stone has many marks in various directions, and is, like all the Binstead stone, full of holes. Five lines can with difficulty be made out, three on the right (as looked at) and two on the left. There is no line in the position of the noon-line. Owing to the height at which the dial is placed and the weathered condition of the stone, the photo taken shows no details. The south wall of the tower faces about S. 40° E.

HERRIARD. Visited July 15, 1924. Nine dials.

There are a most interesting series of dials, eight in number, on the south face of a clasping buttress on the south-east angle of the nave. The church was built about 1200 and was much repaired in 1876–7. The buttresses are original and quite Norman in character, being wide and of slight projection.

All these eight dials face due south, and the style-hole of the highest one is 71 inches from the ground and the lowest 30 inches. (Photos on Plates VII and VIII.)

1. This dial is at the west end of the fourth course of stones from the ground. It is a very distinct dial and consists simply of a style-hole and three well-marked holes from 4 to 5 inches away from it. The style-hole is about $\frac{1}{2}$ inch wide and rather deeper. There are no lines or circle. The holes are placed almost horizontally, one vertically beneath the style-hole and the other two on the western side of it. (See Analysis, p. 119. Photos on Plate VII.)

2. Dial at east end of fourth course. Style-hole is $\frac{1}{2}$ inch wide and 1 inch deep. No circle. There are three distinct lines, a vertical one and a line on each side of it. Above and below the eastern line there are parts of a faintly cut line. The lines differ in length, the longest being 6 to 7 inches. (See Analysis, p. 119. Photos on Plates VII and VIII.)

3. Dial at east end of fifth course. The style-hole, blocked, was in the mortar joint. Vertically below it is a large hole with a line on each side of it, but not very clearly marked on the east. To the west are three clear lines, each ending in a hole, and between each of these lines there is another line, but these two lines do not continue up to the style-hole. The lines are from 5 to 6 inches in length and there is no circle. (See Analysis, p. 121. Photos on Plates VII and VIII.)

4. Dial in the middle of sixth course. There are five lines, all in the western quadrant, the vertical line being very faint and the western one the clearest. They all end in holes and there is no circle. A clear dial, but not deeply cut. (See Analysis, p. 121. Photos on Plates VII and VIII.)

4A. On the right or east of the above and close to it

there are the remains of another dial, a well-marked small style-hole and parts of a complete circle.

5. Dial on east end of ninth course. Style-hole is large. There are ten lines or parts of lines at regular intervals radiating downwards and about 5 inches long. Perhaps there are several lines radiating upwards. (See Analysis, p. 122. Photos on Plate VII.)

6. Dial in centre of ninth course on the next stone to the west of No. 5. The style-hole is blocked. Perhaps there is a circle or part of a circle of small holes, and this is clearly seen in the lower eastern quadrant, which is divided into six equal parts by the holes, but the lines are indistinct. The lines are clearer in the lower western quadrant, which was probably divided in the same manner. If there were any lines or holes in the upper half, they have now disappeared. The vertical line ends in a large hole. (See Analysis, p. 123. Photos on Plate VII.)

7. Dial on tenth course. The style-hole is large and blocked. In the lower western quadrant there is a segment of a circle composed of a number of very small holes. No lines. (Photos on Plate VII.)

8. Dial on east jamb of south doorway, an inverted dial. According to the Victoria County History, *Hants*, the original south doorway has completely disappeared, and the present south doorway in the modern west tower was formerly the north doorway of the nave. How can this dial be accounted for ? It is not likely to have been cut on a north doorway, and there is distinct evidence that it did not originally occupy its present position, in that on arriving at the church at 11 a.m., the sun was observed not to be shining on it, it being in the shadow of a projection of the nave.

Perhaps it is on a stone which originally did form part of the south doorway which is said to have completely disappeared. Inverted dials are so constantly found on portions of a church which are *known* to have been moved, that a dial in such a position may almost be taken as a proof that the structure on which it is incised has been removed from elsewhere. It would seem as if the masons, when removing a doorway, for instance, from one position to another in a church, if it had a dial incised upon it, almost invariably reset the dial in an inverted position, and if the stone on which it was cut contained any architectural detail, such as a chamfer, making it impossible simply to turn the stone upside-down in the same jamb, in such a case the stone was transferred from one side of the doorway to the opposite jamb. The present south doorway here is of two moulded orders with a dog-tooth label and nook-shafts with foliate capitals.

The dial now faces due south, and the style-hole is partly in the mortar joint and partly in the stone ; it is $33\frac{1}{2}$ inches from the ground. From it five lines radiate upwards and are 4 inches long. There is no circle, and on the left-hand side, as the dial now is, are a number of holes and a cross-line, but they do not seem to be connected with the dial.

HOUGHTON. Visited June 1, 1925. One dial.

This dial is on the south-east angle of the south aisle. This aisle, according to the Victoria County History, dates from *c.* 1200. The style-hole, blocked, is about 57 inches from the bottom of the ditch on this side of the church, but only about 30 inches above the surrounding ground. There are seventeen lines to be seen, some very faint. The radii are about 4 inches long.

It faces S. 9° E., and is a large, easily seen dial, many of the lines being deeply cut, but the workmanship is not good. (Photo, Plate VIII.)

HURSTBORNE PRIORS. Visited July 18, 1924. One dial.

There is one dial here on the west jamb of the thirteenth-century (blocked) priest's doorway on the south of the chancel. It faces due south. The style-hole, blocked, is 56 inches from the ground. Part of a circle in the lower half. No holes. The lines all radiate downwards; they are numerous and in many cases appear to be double. (Photo, Plate VIII.)

HURSTBORNE TARRANT. Visited September 4, 1922, and July 17, 1924. One dial.

This dial is on the east jamb of the easternmost window (a double lancet) on the south of the chancel. According to the Victoria County History, *Hants*, this chancel was practically rebuilt in 1890, but the thirteenth-century windows were retained, the heads of the lights, of ogee shape, being modern.

The dial, having a blocked style-hole, is about 7 feet from the ground and faces S. 2° or 3° E. Part of a circle can be seen on the west side, and all the lines radiate downwards. There is a vertical line and four lines to the west and four to the east of it. They measure about 4 or 5 inches.

IDSWORTH. Visited June 16, 1925. Two dials.

This little church is of much interest to the genuine ecclesiologist, and the late thirteenth-century wall-paintings representing St. Hubert taming the Lycanthrope and The Martyrdom of St. John the Baptist should on no account escape attention.

The church dates from the twelfth century, and the walling on the north side is of regularly set flint-work with no quoins at the angles, but in the sixteenth century a south aisle was added with masonry of coarser rubble with sandstone quoins.

It is on one of these sandstone quoins at the south-west angle of the south aisle that the dial is incised. It faces S. 3° W.

The style-hole, in the stone, is 58 inches from the ground, and is not at right angles to the surface. A straight style fixed in it would project outwards and to the east.

The vertical line is the longest, 8½ to 9 inches long, and ends in a hole. Of the two horizontal lines, the right-hand one (east) slopes upwards. Between the vertical and horizontal lines on the left (west) are five lines and on the right (east) four lines.

Several of the lines have holes on them, not always at the ends, and these holes are placed in an indefinite circle.

A photo was taken, and in this on the quoin next above a second dial is to be seen, which was not noticed at the time. It consists of only three lines, a horizontal one to the left (west), a vertical one, and between them another with a style-hole at the junction.

It is but seldom that any date can be assigned to a dial, but it would seem that these two cannot be earlier than the sixteenth century. This is very late, but this church has no clock and probably never had one, and it stands in the middle of a field in a very isolated spot. It is on such a church that a dial might be expected to be useful long after the time when clocks had come into general use in less remote districts. (Photo, Plate IX.)

KIMPTON. Visited July 16, 1925. One dial and a doubtful one.

There is a dial here on a large quoin at the south-east angle of the south transept, and, according to the Victoria County History, *Hants*, this was built in the latter part of the fourteenth century.

The style-hole is 43 inches from the ground. The radii measure to the holes 2½ inches. Aspect, S. 10° W.

It is an imperfect dial with a large style-hole. On the left (west) side there are some lines, four of which end in holes, and in the right (east) lower quadrant some holes and two lines which extend beyond the holes.

There is also a somewhat doubtful dial on another stone a little to the west of the south-east angle of the transept. The style-hole is 81 inches from the ground and is very small. There appear to be three lines in the lower half.

KING'S SOMBORNE.   Visited with the Hants Field Club,
    June 13, 1923.

On this church there are four dials and perhaps others.

Two dials are situated, one above the other, on the east jamb of the fourth window from the east in the south aisle wall. The south aisle was added to the nave in the thirteenth century and was extended eastwards to form a chapel on the south of the chancel in the fourteenth century. There are in this south aisle wall six windows, each of two trefoiled lights, three of which are modern, and the other three probably date from early in the fourteenth century.

The window, fourth from the east (one of the three ancient ones), on which these dials are incised is inserted into an old doorway, the blocked portion of which is filled in with stonework, and there is stonework under the other two ancient windows, but the rest of the wall is of flint work.

1. Of these dials, the *upper* is the more distinct, and it faces S. 27° W. The style-hole is 51½ inches from the ground. The dial is 5 inches in diameter and has

twenty-four lines, each of which ends in a small hole. (A good photo on Plate IX.)

2. The *lower dial*, which is on the same stone, is much less distinct, and measures 4½ inches in diameter, while the style-hole is 47 inches from the ground. There seem to be about six lines, three of which are in the upper half and the most distinct is in the lower east quadrant. The dial appears as if squeezed into the space between the upper dial and the lower edge of the stone. (Photo, Plate IX.)

3. The *third dial* is on the west jamb of the same window, but faces due south. The stone on which it is cut is much broken away, but the remains of the style-hole are about 51 inches from the ground. The whole dial is very imperfect, but it probably had twenty-four lines, some at least of which ended in small holes.

4. The *fourth dial* is cut on a soft stone with a smooth surface on the south of the south-east corner of the chancel. It faces S. 16° W., is 4 inches in diameter, and the style-hole, which is large, is 55 inches from the ground. It is surrounded by a circle and has ten lines in the lower half, five of which end in distinct holes, and two lines in the upper half. This dial is peculiar in that none of the lines are very straight and most of them are distinctly curved.

LAVERSTOKE. Visited July 14, 1924. Two dials.

The old parish church of St. Mary the Virgin stands in the grounds of Laverstoke House, and is now used as the mortuary chapel for the Portal family. Parts of the building are probably of pre-Conquest date.

1. This dial is on the large irregular lintel over the blocked doorway on the *north* of the nave. As there is no doubt that this is a primitive sundial, the inference is that the doorway was once on the opposite side of the

church, because the dial would be useless in its present position. The style-hole is in about the centre of the lintel and retains a small piece of style, of iron, with the red stain on the stone all round it. It is 88 inches from the ground. There are five lines, one of which is not so distinct as the others; they are about 6 inches long and are enclosed in a segment of a circle. The whole dial is enclosed in a deeply incised upright parallelogram. (See Analysis, p. 124. Photo, Plate X.)

2. This dial is interesting because of its peculiar orientation, and it is unfortunate that so little of it remains. It is on the *east* face of the south-east angle of the nave and faces due east. The stone is much weathered and the dial very indistinct. The style-hole, blocked, is $48\frac{1}{2}$ inches from the ground, and about ten lines, radiating in all directions, can be deciphered, four of which end in holes. The radii measure $4\frac{1}{2}$ inches. The Victoria County History says the eastern angles of the nave have quoins of very early character, probably of pre-Conquest date. It is possible therefore that this dial, although facing due east, is *in situ*.

MARTIN. Visited July 18, 1923. Four dials.

There are three dials here, which are of great interest because of their peculiar orientation. They are found on the corner buttresses of the south transept, which dates from *c.* 1340.

1. A dial on a buttress placed diagonally at the south-west corner of the south transept. It faces S. 35° W. The stone is covered with lichen, but the lines are fairly clear except in the upper part. The style-hole is 59 inches from the ground, and the lines, seventeen of which can be deciphered, radiate in all directions and are 3 inches long. (Photo, Plate X.)

2. On the next stone below the above is another very similar dial, but either on account of its age or of the overgrowth of lichen, it is much more difficult to be clearly seen. The style-hole is 48 inches from the ground and the dial measures $5\frac{3}{4}$ inches across. Thirteen lines can be deciphered, but three of these, the only ones seen in the upper half, are very faint. Faces S. 35° W. (Photo, Plate X.)

3. This dial is on the corresponding diagonal buttress at the south-east corner of the south transept. There are perhaps two dials here, but one is very faint and only the style-hole is plain. The stone is overgrown with lichen. This dial faces S. 36° E., the style-hole is $45\frac{1}{2}$ inches from the ground, and the radii measure $4\frac{1}{4}$ inches long. It is quite unlike the two dials on the corresponding buttress, having five lines only, all of which radiate downwards and none of them is vertical.

The earliest church at Martin of which there are traces belonged to the first half of the twelfth century. The chancel was rebuilt about the middle of the thirteenth century, when the west tower was added. The chancel was lengthened eastwards early in the fourteenth century, and the south transept dates from c. 1340. (Victoria County History, *Hants.*) The diagonal buttresses to the south transepts, in view of all these alterations, may have been built of re-used stones, and the dials on them, considering how unsuitable they seem to be for their orientation, may formerly have occupied different positions.

4. This dial is on a fifteenth-century buttress on the south-east of the tower near the porch. It faces S. 22° W. The style-hole is 57 inches from the ground and the radii measure 3 inches. The photo hardly conveys a correct idea of this dial, for a rough sketch

made at the same time shows thirteen lines, most of which end in small holes.

MONK SHERBORNE. All Saints'. Visited July 16, 1924. One dial.

The dial here is on the south-east angle of the nave and faces due south. The wall is of early twelfth-century date. The style-hole, filled with plaster, is 42 inches from the ground. It is not a distinct dial, but eight lines can be made out, the two central ones, neither of which is vertical, being composed of a series of dots. One line, on the west, is above the horizontal.

NEWTON VALENCE. Visited June 17, 1925. Two dials.

The church here dates from *c.* 1220, and both dials are situated on the east jamb of the priest's door on the south of the chancel. This doorway has a pointed arch of two chamfered orders, and is now covered by a modern vestry, but previous to the building of this, it was external.

The *upper dial* faces S. 28° W. and has a style-hole in the stone 57 inches from the ground. The vertical line, which is the longest, measures $3\frac{1}{4}$ inches. To the right (east) of this are three lines, which are short on account of the plaster on the wall here. On the left (west) there are five lines, the one next to the vertical line ending in a small hole. There are no horizontal lines.

The *lower dial* faces S. 28° W., and its style-hole, which is square, contains the broken-off stump of the style, probably an iron one. It is $45\frac{1}{2}$ inches from the ground. There are a vertical and two horizontal lines, and between them on the right (east) four lines and on the left (west) three lines.

In consequence of the light in the vestry being very deficient, a good photo was impossible.

PENTON MEWSEY.   Visited July 18, 1924.   Two dials.

This church dates from 1340 to 1350.   The walls are of faced flint with large ashlar quoins.

1. This dial is on a quoin at the south-west angle of the nave. It faces S. 20° W. The style-hole is in a masonry joint and is 57 inches from the ground.   There are five lines of $2\frac{1}{4}$ inches in length, and of these three, viz. the vertical line and one on each side of it, are very clearly cut.   On each side of the eastern line there is another line but it is not so conspicuous.   No circle and no holes. (See Analysis, p. 130.   Photo, Plate XI.)

2. At the south-east angle of the nave there appears to be another dial.   The style-hole is in a joint and is 51 inches from the ground.   Perhaps five lines can be seen from 2 to $2\frac{1}{2}$ inches long.   A doubtful dial.

PRESTON CANDOVER.   Visited July 15, 1924.   One dial.

This dial is on the lowest stone of the west jamb of the south doorway of the chancel.   The church, all but the chancel, which is now used as a mortuary chapel, was burnt down in 1884.   Dr. Cox says it had particularly valuable pre-Conquest work.   The doorway is blocked and has chamfered jambs.   The head is round and of later date than the jambs.   It is not certain, but probably the dial is *in situ*.

The dial is placed very low, the style-hole being on a level with the ground, but 12 inches above the bottom of the ditch round the church.   It is contained in a complete circle of about 6 inches in diameter, but it is longer perpendicularly than from side to side. The style-hole is large and 1½ inches deep. Thirteen lines can be seen, all in the lower half. There are no holes, and the stone is much damaged by weather. (Photo, Plate XI.)

QUARLEY. Visited July 16, 1925. One good dial and two very doubtful ones.

The dial is on the west jamb of the south window of the nave, to the east of the doorway. This window dates from early in the fifteenth century (Victoria County History). The style-hole, which is blocked, the plaster extending for a considerable and irregular distance, is 68 inches from the ground, i.e. from the bottom of the ditch. The diameter is 4¼ inches.

In the upper eastern quadrant the lines have disappeared, but what remains of the dial is very good and about twenty-two lines and holes can be plainly seen, although they are not deeply cut.

Below the lower vertical line are four holes set in a lozenge shape. The aspect is S. 3° W.

From the appearance of the western half of the dial, which is perfect and shows thirteen lines each ending in a hole, there is no doubt that this was originally a complete wheel dial.

On the east jamb of the same window there are two very doubtful dials.

ROCKBOURNE. Visited July 20, 1923. One dial.

This dial, which is very distinct, is on a fifteenth-century buttress on the south of the south chapel. It faces due south and is about 5 feet 4 inches from the ground. It consists of a style-hole and thirteen lines placed at equal distances apart and all in the lower half.

Each line ends in a hole, but there is no circular line, and four of the lowest lines extend considerably beyond the holes. The second line from the top on the west also has a second hole outside the first one. The lines measure 4 inches to the holes.

ROWNER. Visited August 31, 1925. Two dials.

There are two dials here on adjoining quoins at the south-east angle of the old chancel, which was built in the first half of the twelfth century. They face S. 1° W.

The top dial has a style-hole in and below a mortar-joint and 70 inches from the ground. There are nine lines, four on each side of a vertical line, all of which seem to have been scratched over recently. The noon-line, 5 inches long, inclines a little to the east below, and all the lines are of about the same length and are enclosed in a half-circle, the two upper ones on the west extending on to the stone immediately to the westward. There are no dots or holes.

The lower dial, on the quoin below the upper one, is indistinct. It has a large style-hole, blocked, and is 60 inches from the ground. Five lines can be seen with traces of others, and there are indications of a complete circle. All the lines now visible are in the lower half, a vertical line and three to the west of it (the three lower ending in holes) and one line in the eastern quadrant. (Photo showing both, Plate XI.)

ST. MARY BOURNE. Visited August 24, 1922, with the Hants Field Club. One dial.

The south chapel of this church seems to have been built in the last half of the fourteenth century, and it is on a buttress of this chapel, east of the south porch, that the dial is situated. The stone is very soft and most of the surface has scaled off. It is a large dial, the lines, about eight in number, all radiating downwards and measuring from 8 to 10 inches, and it faces due south. No photo taken.

SHERBORNE ST. JOHN. Visited July 16, 1924. Five dials.

1. This dial is on the summit of the round-headed arch of the south doorway, which dates from *c.* 1150. It is now covered by a sixteenth-century porch. The dial faces due south, and the lines, which are deeply cut and of unequal length, extend over five voussoirs. A small pipe (? for electric wire) runs down the key-stone to the west of the vertical line. The style-hole, now blocked, is in the mortar-line and is about 95 inches from the ground. The vertical line, which is cut on the key-stone, and is not in a mortar-line, measures $7\frac{1}{2}$ inches, and inclines slightly to the east below. On the west of the vertical line there are three lines, the uppermost of which is by far the longest and measures 18 inches or more. There are two lines on the east of the vertical line and these measure 10 to 12 inches. Possibly also there is a horizontal line on each side, but these are not easy to decipher. There is no circle and there are no holes. (See Analysis, p. 131, and cover photograph.)

2. This wheel-dial is on the east side of the south porch doorway. The porch was built in 1533, according to an inscription over it, but the dial may be on a reused stone. From the evidence afforded by the dial itself, the lines being much deeper and clearer in the lower half than the upper, one would be inclined to think that it had not been inverted, and if that is so perhaps the dial is *in situ*. The porch is built of bricks with stone quoins and the dial is on one of the latter.

The style-hole, $\frac{1}{2}$ inch wide and $\frac{1}{2}$ inch deep, is 37 inches from the ground, and there is a perfect circle $7\frac{1}{4}$ inches in diameter. There are seventeen lines, some of which are clear incisions and some mere scratches, and the curious point to be observed is the two parallel lines above and below the style-hole, but they are not quite symmetrically placed. It is possible that straight lines such as these might be intended to mark both sides of the shadow at noon and take the place of one line marking the middle of the shadow.

The dial faces due south. There are several holes outside the circle, but they do not seem to be connected with the dial. (Photo, Plate VI.)

3. This dial is on a quoin at the south-west angle of the nave, the date of the wall being uncertain, but perhaps c. 1150. This is a symmetrical dial of good workmanship situated about 9 feet from the ground and facing due south. The style-hole is contained in a perfect circle, which is divided equally by a horizontal and a vertical line. The upper half of the circle has only this one line, but each quadrant of the lower half is divided into three equal parts by two lines. The lower vertical line is continued below the circle, the projecting part being marked by a cross. Crosses just like this, though not quite in the same position, are characteristic of Saxon dials, but the division of the day into six equal parts, as is here shown, is certainly not a pre-Conquest feature. Without being dogmatic and taking into account the general good workmanship and symmetry of the dial and the little cross, one cannot help surmising that this and similar dials are very ancient ones. There are no holes. (See Analysis, p. 132. Photo, Plate XV.)

4. This dial is on the south-east angle of the chancel, which was rebuilt in the middle of the fourteenth century. It is one of those peculiar dials (like the one at

Upham), with deeply cut wedge-shaped lines, and it is very unfortunate that a water-pipe has been fixed immediately in front of and close to it, a photograph thus being impossible. The style-hole is deep and 1½ inches wide and is 45 inches from the ground. There is no circle. The lines, six in number, and 3 inches long, all radiate downwards, and are deep and wide below, tapering upwards to the style-hole. It faces due south. As we are unable, at present, to date dials by their general characteristics, we must remain uncertain as to whether this dial was cut after the rebuilding of the chancel in the middle of the fourteenth century or whether it is an earlier dial on a reused stone from the former chancel.

5. This dial is on the *east* face of the south-east angle of the chancel, which was rebuilt in the middle of the fourteenth century. The stone is much weathered and the lines very shallow and hardly perceptible. The style-hole is very shallow and 22 inches from the ground. Perhaps ten lines can be seen from 2 to 3½ inches long, all but one radiating downwards. It faces due east, and the whole dial appears to be tilted up to the north. No holes and no circle. (Photo, Plate VI.)

This dial, like No. 4, may be on a reused stone.

SOBERTON.   ? A dial.

At the east end of the north chapel or vestry of this church there is a window of two trefoiled ogee lights, and between the two ogee arches and above the central mullion there is a circle incised on a flat stone. The circle consists of two lines, one within the other, and close together. In the centre is a hole and at a little distance from this a smaller circle. There are no lines or holes (but it may have been painted), and it faces towards the east.

This part of the church and this window are dated
c. 1330.   This must be accounted a doubtful dial.

Steventon.   Visited July 14, 1924.   Four dials.

1. This dial is on the south jamb of the *west* doorway,
which dates from *c.* 1200.   Probably this doorway was
once in the south wall of the nave.   The style-hole is partly
in the line of mortar and partly in the stone.   There are
some doubtful holes, and eleven or twelve lines, those on
the east, about 5 inches long, being longer than those on
the west.   Directly below the style-hole the stone is
much damaged, but perhaps there were two vertical
lines descending one from each side of the style-hole.

The remaining three dials are on the south face of the
south-west angle of the nave, and this wall dates from
c. 1200.   They all face S. 12° W.

2. This dial has a very large style-hole, 60 inches from
the ground.   It has two horizontal lines and a lower
vertical one, and, including these, thirteen lines in the
lower half.   Many of the lines end in holes, and some of
the former are much more clearly cut than others.   The
radii measure about $4\frac{1}{2}$ inches.   Above the horizontal
lines there are three lines fairly definite and perhaps some
others.   If there is a circle, it is very faint.   (See
Analysis, p. 132.   Photo, Plate XIII.)   A very interesting dial.

3. If this is a dial, it is of a quite unusual type.   It is
situated below and to the east of No. 2.   It has no
circle, and the style-hole, which is small, is 53 inches
from the ground.   It measures $2\frac{1}{2}$ inches across.

It consists of eight radiating, equidistant lines each
ending in a hole.   These are very good, clearly cut lines,
but in addition there are four other lines, not so strongly
marked and not ending in holes, and they are placed one
on each side of the eastern horizontal line and one on

each side of the lower vertical line. The dial is
therefore divided diagonally, the western and upper half
having four equal divisions and the lower and eastern
half having eight equal divisions. (Photo, Plate XIII.)

4. This dial is on a stone two courses below No. 2.
The style-hole, fairly large, is 45 inches from the ground,
and there is an indistinct circle perhaps all round.
Seven lines can be seen, and there may be others.

STOCKBRIDGE. Visited May 1922. One dial, in a reversed position.

This dial is now in the new church, erected 1863, but
various portions of the old church, of early thirteenth- or
possibly late twelfth-century date, have been preserved
in it. Among these removed portions is a two-light
window now at the west end of the north aisle. It is a
double lancet of the early geometrical style with a circle
over. The window has been restored, and the Victoria
County History, *Hants*, says it is of late twelfth-century
date, while, on the other hand, Dr. J. Charles Cox, in
the *Hants Little Guide*, says it is temp. Edward I.

The dial is on one of the stones forming part of the
right-hand jamb of this window and it is upside-down.
There is a style-hole with a vertical line above, and on
each side of this four radiating lines. It is too high for
a photo or for measurement.

Dr. Cox says, " One of the stones of the right-hand
jamb of this window is moulded from an undoubted
Saxon sundial in a reversed position, a relic of a pre-
Norman stone church on the old site."

It is quite unlike the dials which we now know to be
of Saxon date, such as those found at Corhampton,
Warnford, Winchester, Daglingworth, Kirkdale, etc.,
etc., and is quite certainly an ordinary dial of the kind
which is now under consideration.

It is a curious fact that many dials, at least in Hampshire, which are on windows or doorways and which are known to have been removed from some other position, have been inverted.

STOKE CHARITY.   There are six dials here and perhaps two more.

Five of these dials are incised (three on one stone) on the east jamb of the south window of the nave.   This is a two-light window of *c.* 1320, the tracery having been repaired.   All these dials face due south.

1. This dial, the upper one, is very indistinct and overgrown with lichen.   Five lines can be seen in the lower western quadrant.   It is too high up to be measured.

2. This dial and the next two are all close together on the same stone, which is two stones below No. 1. It has a circle and a large style-hole, which is about 2 yards above the drain which here runs round the church, but the bottom of the drain is much below the level of the ground beyond.   Therefore these four lower dials are not much higher than an observer's eyes.   The diameter of the circle is 5 inches, and probably there were originally radiating lines all round, but four or five confused lines in the lower western quadrant are the most easily distinguished now.   (Good photo, Plate XIII.)

3. A clear dial, having six lines in the lower western quadrant, the three lower ones ending in distinct holes. The upper three lines are not so clear and they also probably end in holes.   The style-hole is in the circle surrounding the dial above, Dial No. 2.   The radii are 3 inches long.   (See Analysis, p. 137.   Photo, Plate XIII.)

4. A small dial within a circle 2 inches in diameter. There are three lines ending in holes in the lower western

quadrant and parts of two lines in the upper half, and the photo shows traces of other lines and holes. (Plate XIII.)

5. This dial is on the next stone below the one on which the last three are cut. It is 3 inches in diameter, but has no circle. Eleven lines, including the two vertical ones, can be made out on the eastern side, and five lines on the western side. A small, well-marked hole is to be seen above the vertical line.

6. This dial is on the *west* jamb of the same window and also faces due south. It is 3 inches in diameter, but has no distinct circle. The style-hole is less than 2 yards from the drain and is rather below the level of the observer's eyes. Twelve lines radiate from the style-hole at fairly equal angles all round, and of these four in the western half are very well cut, and in the lower eastern quadrant the upper of the two lines appears to be double. (See Analysis, p. 138. Good photo, Plate XIII.)

TIMSBURY. Visited April 14, 1922. One dial.

The dial on this church appears to a casual observer to be a one-line dial, but the photograph shows four lines, and there may be others under the lichen which covers the stone. It is situated on the south of the south-east angle of the chancel and faces due south. The nave of this church was probably built in the thirteenth century, but the chancel seems to have been rebuilt in the fifteenth century. The wall of the chancel is composed of flint and rubble, but has ashlar stones at the angles, and the dial is on one of these.

The style-hole, blocked, must have been in a joint, and this has been re-pointed, and is about $55\frac{1}{2}$ inches from the ground. The four lines, which are all in the lower half, are 4 inches long, and there is no circle.

The easternmost line may be intended to be vertical, but it probably slopes to the right (east) at its lower end. (See Analysis, p. 139. Photo, Plate XIV.)

UPHAM. Visited June 1922. One dial.

This is a dial of a very unusual and rare type. Dom Ethelbert Horne, in his book on *Primitive Sundials*, gives an illustration of one. It is cut on a quoin, probably of Binstead stone, at the south-east angle of the chancel, and the Victoria County History, *Hants*, says that these quoins are of thirteenth-century character.

The style-hole is 42 inches from the ground, but the peculiar character of the dial is seen in the lines, which are deep and wedge-shaped, and broad and wide at the circumference, tapering to a line as they approach the style-hole. There are seven or eight of these lines, all in the lower half, about 2 inches long, and there is no circle. The wall faces S. 20° E. (Photo, Plate XIV.)

UP NATELEY. Visited July 15, 1924. One dial.

.This dial is at the east end of the sill of the south-east window of the chancel. The Victoria County History, *Hants*, says that the chancel was built in 1844, but this window appears to be of fifteenth-century date. It consists of two trefoiled lights under a square label and is probably a reused window inserted when the chancel was built.

The dial faces now S. 32° E. The line of junction between the chamfer and the face of the sill forms the horizontal line and the style-hole is in this line. The stone is cracked in the upper part, and the upper and eastern parts of the dial are broken away.

The style-hole is now 58 inches from the ground, and is $\frac{1}{2}$ an inch wide and $\frac{3}{4}$ of an inch deep. Eleven clearly cut lines can be seen. The half-circle is double in parts and the radii measure $3\frac{1}{2}$ and 4 inches to the inner and outer circles. There are no holes.

The lines on this dial are cut with a remarkable degree of accuracy, the angles formed being always very nearly 15°. (See Analysis, p. 139. Photo, Plate XIV.)

NORTH WALTHAM. Visited July 14, 1924. One dial.

This dial is on the west jamb of the south doorway of the chancel, the priest's doorway. The Victoria County History says that this is a modern doorway, but it contains some reused old stones, especially in the lower part, and the dial is on one of these. The doorway in its original state probably dates from c. 1300, and it seems likely that the dial is in its original position.

It consists of a large style-hole, not more than $\frac{1}{2}$ inch deep and $33\frac{1}{2}$ inches from the ground. The rest is very difficult to make out. There are, perhaps, four or five holes arranged in a semicircle and two or three faint lines which are about $2\frac{1}{4}$ inches long.

WARBLINGTON. Visited June 27, 1924. One dial.

The dial is on the west jamb of the south-east window of the south aisle and the western part of the dial is plastered over. The part that can be seen consists of a style-hole, a horizontal line, and three other lines radiating downwards to the east. The longest line is 5 inches.

The style-hole, 75 inches from the ground, contains soft metal, perhaps lead. The dial faces S. 2° E.

WARNFORD. Visited August 11, 1923. Four dials.

A well-preserved Saxon sundial is to be seen here

over the south doorway and under the porch, and the
points of difference between this type and the dials
now under consideration are very obvious. It has been
described elsewhere.[1] The south porch probably dates
from early in the thirteenth century, although some
writers call it Transitional Norman. On the quoins of
its plain, pointed, outer arch there are four dials, two on
each side of the entrance.

1. The upper dial on the east of the entrance has seven
well-marked lines, including a vertical line, and on the
west a horizontal line (which, however, slopes somewhat
upwards), and between these there are four radiating
lines, the third line from the vertical being very deeply
cut. Between this well-cut line and the one above it
there is a hole. On the east side of the dial there is one
well-marked line with a faint line on each side of and
close to it. These lines measure about $2\frac{1}{2}$ inches. The
style-hole is 62 inches from the ground and there is no
circle. It faces S. 15° E. (See Analysis, p. 140.
Photo, Plate XIV.)

2. The lower dial on the east side of the entrance is on
the next stone below and has a complete circle and
twenty-four lines radiating all round, at fairly equal
angles, from the central style-hole, which is 54 inches
from the ground. The middle line in the lower west
quadrant is in this dial also the most deeply cut. The
circle is 7 inches in diameter and has perhaps three
holes in the upper part of its circumference. It faces
S. 15° E. (Photo, Plate XIV.)

3 and 4. These two dials are on the west side of the
entrance; they are very indistinct, the style-holes alone
being marked. The western one is contained in a circle
8 inches in diameter with a style-hole 48 inches from the
ground.

[1] P. 18

WINCHFIELD. Visited July 15, 1924. Two dials.

The church of St. Mary exhibits exceedingly rich details of late Norman work. The chancel arch, 6 feet wide, is the narrowest late Norman chancel archway in all England, and has on its capital a splendid specimen of the naturalistic foliage of the last quarter of the twelfth century, an unfolding fern-leaf. (Bond.) The various capitals in the church exhibit almost every variety of foliate and scalloped capitals of Norman architecture.

There are two dials on one stone in the east jamb of the doorway of the south porch. This porch is stated by the Victoria County History to be an erection of late fifteenth- or early sixteenth-century date. This stone has probably been reused and inverted, one point, which seems to favour this view, being that there is in the lower left corner the letter A in an upside-down position.

1. The upper dial has a large style-hole 34 inches from the ground. There probably was a complete circle, but the stone is much weathered, and it can only now be seen in parts. Most of the lines radiate upwards, and two or three of these are deeply cut, the vertical line being especially clear. There are faint indications of some lines radiating downwards. From the well-marked character of the upper lines in comparison with the others it seems probable that this is an inverted dial on an old reused stone.

2. The lower dial on the same stone (? inverted) is small and indistinct. The style-hole is 28 inches from the ground, and is surrounded by a circle 3 inches in diameter. There are a number of faint lines which appear to radiate in all directions, and are, perhaps, more distinct in the lower than in the upper half. (Photo, Plate XV.)

WONSTON. Visited April 10, 1923. Three dials.

There are three dials on this church and all are incised on the south doorway, which was built *c.* 1150 and is now covered by a modern wooden porch. Two dials are on the west jamb, one above the other. They face due south.

The upper dial (1), very imperfect, has about sixteen lines or parts of lines radiating all round a rather large style-hole, which is 57 inches from the ground. What may be called the noon-line is $2\frac{1}{2}$ inches long, but the lines in the lower and western part of the dial are much longer than those in the upper and eastern part. The stone is much damaged, probably from exposure to the weather.

2. The lower dial is not quite so much damaged. Nine lines can be seen, all in the lower half, and the noon-line is $2\frac{1}{4}$ inches long. The style-hole is 49 inches from the ground. The photos taken were not good ones, as the light under the porch is very bad.

3. The third dial is on the east jamb of the same south doorway and faces due south. The style-hole is 51 inches from the ground and the noon-line is $2\frac{1}{2}$ inches long. There are seven or perhaps eight lines, four in the west lower quadrant, two or three in the east lower quadrant, and one vertical line. This dial, although damaged, is not so imperfect as the other two. (Photo, Plate XV.)

ARRETON, ISLE OF WIGHT. Visited October 8, 1925. One dial.

The remains of a dial are to be seen on the east jamb of the south doorway. The style-hole contains the broken-off stump of a metal style. Two lines are visible, both in the lower eastern quadrant, and part of a circle in the lower half.

There is an inserted stone in the south wall of the south chapel to the west of the easternmost window. This *might* be the remains of a dial, possibly of Saxon date. A style-hole can be seen, but nothing else remains.

BINSTEAD, ISLE OF WIGHT. Visited October 1925. One dial.

The dial here is plainly seen, although there is some lichen over it. It is situated at the south-east corner of the chancel, which dates from *c.* 1150, and is not on a corner quoin but on the next stone to the west of it. It faces S. 3° W.

The style-hole, in the stone, is 63 inches from the ground. The circle, a complete one, has a diameter of 7½ inches, and is divided by vertical and horizontal lines into four quadrants. Each quadrant is again divided by three lines into four parts, each line marking 1½ hours. These lines are not all equally visible.

The lower eastern quadrant, which has a patch of lichen over it, seems to be further subdivided near the vertical line. (Photo, Plate I.)

CALBORNE, ISLE OF WIGHT. Visited October 12, 1925. Two dials.

Here there are two dials on the same stone in the east jamb of the south, priest's, door. The doorway has a pointed arch with a plain chamfer which stops about 1 foot from the ground. Thirteenth century. Aspect, S. 13° W. (Photo, Plate XII.)

1. Dial on the left, or west. The style-hole is small, and in the lower western quadrant there are three holes with very faint lines extending towards the style-hole. There are faint indications of a horizontal line on this side. No vertical line or hole can be seen. In the lower eastern quadrant one line ending in a hole can be

seen with difficulty. The style-hole, in the stone, is 60 inches from the ground and the radii measure 2 inches.

2. Dial on the right, or east. The style-hole, in the stone, is 1 inch deep and 59½ inches from the ground, and is surrounded by lichen, which obscures the whole dial. In the lower western quadrant there are four holes, the highest of which has a line. These holes are about 4 inches from the style-hole. Directly below the style-hole a short vertical line is seen ending in a hole, and in the eastern quadrant two other short lines end in holes. The last three holes mentioned are only about 2½ inches from the style-hole. Probably much more of this dial could be seen if the lichen were removed.

SHALFLEET, ISLE OF WIGHT. Visited October 12, 1925.
     One dial.

The dial is on the east jamb of the south doorway under a fifteenth-century porch. The doorway, which dates from the last half of the thirteenth century, has a pointed arch with two continuous rolls, one of which ends in a base. The hoodmould is deeply undercut and is stopped by two human heads. The one on the east is much weathered, but that on the west shows a female head with the head-dress of the time of Edward I.

A square of plaster has been, probably recently, removed to expose the eastern part of the dial. Aspect, S. 3° E.

The style-hole is large, in the stone, and 36 inches from the ground. Part of a circle is present in the lower western quadrant. The vertical line ends in a hole, and in the lower western quadrant there are six lines, the upper one being horizontal. The lower eastern quadrant shows two lines, and there would appear to be a short line in the upper eastern quadrant. The radii measure 3½ inches. (Photo, Plate XII.)

YAVERLAND, ISLE OF WIGHT.   Visited October 6, 1925.
   One dial.

This dial is on the west jamb of the enriched south
doorway, which dates from c. 1150, and is now covered by
a modern porch.   It consists of a style-hole in a mortar-
joint and a half-circle, and it faces due south.   Twelve
lines can be seen, all in the lower half, radiating from
the style-hole, four of which are prolonged beyond the
circle.   Style-hole to ground, 51½ inches.   Style-hole
to circumference, 4 inches.   Noon-line, 9 inches long.
(Photo, Plate XV.)

NORTH CERNEY, GLOS.   Visited May 1920 and August
   1922.   Two dials.

The church, remarkable for having incised on its walls
the figures of two large manticoras, has also on the *east*
wall of its south transept what is thought to be a kind
of sundial.   The Rector very kindly pointed this out to
me, and if it is one, it is of the hole-type, having no lines
nor, I believe, any central style-hole.   It is *very* large,
and from its position, size, and general characteristics
quite unlike the dials under consideration.   There are,
however, two ordinary dials here.

1. This dial is on a buttress at the south-west of the
tower.   This buttress, which the Rector says is of fifteenth-
century date and the stone a local oolite, has a small
doorway opening through it, and the dial is on the east
of this.   It has a deeply cut complete circle, which is
double in the lower eastern part, and eight lines all in
the lower half.   It faces due south.   The style-hole,
blocked, is 35¼ inches from the ground, and the diameter
of the circle is 10 inches.   (Good photo, Plate III.)

2. On the west side of the doorway on this same
buttress is a smaller dial.   It consists of a broken circle,
much overgrown with lichen, and 4 inches in diameter

vertically, but as the east side is encroached upon by a joint, the diameter from side to side is $3\frac{1}{2}$ inches. The style-hole is 24 inches from the ground, and the only two lines visible are in the lower eastern quadrant.

BRIDGE SOLLARS, HEREFORD.   Visited March 1921. One dial.

This dial is cut on the apex of a thirteenth-century doorway. It consists of a style-hole, blocked, in a masonry joint, part of a circle in the lower portion, and four lines radiating downwards. It is illustrated in Fr. Horne's book, where he shows most conclusively that it cannot have been constructed before the Early-English doorway was set up. The vertical line is in the masonry joint between the two stones forming the apex of the arch. This, therefore, is a dial, dated to this extent, that it cannot possibly be older than the thirteenth-century doorway on which it is incised.

BARFRESTON, KENT.   Visited September 1923.   Eight dials.

This well-known church with its rich ornamentation ranks with Iffley and Kilpeck as a gem of Norman architecture.   It was built probably in 1081, the material being Caen stone.

The south doorway has three dials on its west jamb and three dials on its east jamb. All these face about S. 10° W.

1. The upper dial on the west jamb has its style-hole in a masonry joint.   It has no circle and consists of three lines, one of which is nearly vertical and the other two are on its western side. (Photo, Plate I.)

2. This dial is below No. 1 on the same block of stone. The style-hole is blocked. There are three lines, each ending in a small hole, two of which are on the western side, and the other has a slight slant to the east. In addition,

above the upper western line there is another, which, however, ends above the style-hole. (Photo, Plate I.)

3. This is a most interesting and deeply cut dial, and is situated on the next stone below No. 2. The style-hole is in a joint, and the irregular semicircle, somewhat pointed below, is cut off on the east by the edge of the jamb of the doorway. The five lines, all in the lower western quadrant, are deeply cut and wedge-shaped, the thin end of the wedge pointing to the style-hole. Outside and below the circular edge, and in a direct vertical line with the style-hole, a well-marked hole is to be seen, and to the westward the next line is continued outside the circle as a faint thin line ending in a small hole. Probably these two features ought to be considered as parts of the dial. This dial may belong to that peculiar type of which Fr. Horne found three examples in Somerset and of which the dial at Upham is a good example. (Photo, Plate I.)

Three dials on the east jamb. They face S. about 10° W. (Plate I.)

4. The upper dial here has a complete circle, the upper part of which is not shown in the photo. There are five lines, all in the lower west quadrant. A very clear dial. (See Analysis, p. 105, and diagram and other information, pp. 91–94. Various Theories.)

5. This dial is on the next stone below No. 4 and the style-hole is in the joint between the two stones. Of the four lines to be seen, there is one not quite vertical, and on the east of this one line and on the west two lines. (See Analysis, p. 106.)

6. The lowest dial on the east jamb is cut on the same stone as No. 5. In comparison with the length of the lines the style-hole is large, and the four clearly cut lines, all in the lower western quadrant, have a rather wedge-shaped appearance. The western line is by far the

longest. There is also on the western side a horizontal line, of quite different character, being thin and indistinct, and drawn below the centre of the style-hole.

The two other dials at this church are incised on quoins at the south-east angle of the nave. They face about S. 10° W. (Plate I.)

7. The upper dial consists of a complete circle containing twenty-four lines, forming a wheel dial. Some of the lines are not very distinct. There is one hole outside the circle in the lower left quadrant. (See Analysis, p. 107.)

8. The lower dial is on the quoin immediately below No. 7, and the style-hole is in the joint. This dial is much weathered, but there is a vertical line, and to the west of it three other lines.

KINLET, SALOP. Visited May 1924. One dial.

This church, celebrated for its monumental effigies, was unfortunately visited on a very wet day. No photo, measurements, etc., could be taken in consequence. The dial is on a fourteenth-century buttress at the eastern part of the south chapel. It is perhaps 7 feet from the ground and consists of a half-circle which has a double line. The stone is much worn and the lines very indistinct, but four lines can be seen on each side of the middle vertical line. None of these eight lines now extends far from the circumference towards the centre.

COMPTON, SURREY. Visited with the Hants Field
    Club, May 23, 1923. Two dials.

1. This dial is on the east jamb of a low-side window in the south wall of the south aisle. The round-headed top of the window is cut out of a single stone. The style-hole is large, and there are five lines radiating downwards—a vertical one, and one on the left or west, and three on the east.

2. This dial is *very* small and the lines very thin. It is on the central mullion of a window, next to, and on the east side of the porch, in the south wall of the south aisle. The lines, four in number, all radiate downwards, and are not more than an inch long, if as much; and the style-hole, if there was one, is closed up.

No photos, measurements, etc., of these dials could be taken.

WOOTTON WARWEN, WARWICKSHIRE. Visited August 7, 1922. One dial.

This very interesting church has a dial which is spoiled by the crumbling away of the stone. It is on the south-east buttress of the south chapel, which is of fourteenth-century date. The style-hole is about 4 feet 9 inches from the ground, and the radii, which are cut on at least three stones, are quite 12 inches long. No photo taken.

DOWNTON, WILTS. Visited March 1923. One large dial, remains of two others.

The dial is on a buttress on the south of the nave between the south doorway and a doorway farther to the east, now blocked. The buttress has two set-offs; the lower one, of much projection, is probably of fourteenth-century date. It is a regular, well-defined dial with a complete circle of a diameter of 17 inches. The style-hole, which is clearly cut, is square, and 94 inches from the ground. The upper half of the dial has one vertical line, and in the lower half are thirteen lines at regular intervals. The dial is not all cut on one stone, the lowest part being continued on the next stone below. It faces due south. (See Analysis, p. 117. Photo, Plate V.)

Below the lower set-off, on the same buttress, are the remains of a second dial.

There is a third dial, very indistinct, on a buttress which forms part of a porch to a doorway. This buttress is on the west side of the south-east doorway.

ODSTOCK, WILTS. Visited March 1923. Two dials.

Both dials are on the west jamb of the south door-way of the nave. The wall here has been plastered over and subsequently scraped, the consequence being that the dials are somewhat spoiled. They face S. 30° E.

1. The upper dial with well-cut lines has a complete circle somewhat indistinct on the east. The style-hole is 40 inches from the ground and is stopped with plaster. There are twelve lines, including two horizontal and two vertical, and in the upper half one line in the east and two lines in the west quadrant, and in the lower half three lines in the east and two (one being a double line) in the west quadrant. The diameter of the circle is $7\frac{3}{4}$ inches.

2. The lower dial is smaller; its complete circle measures $4\frac{1}{2}$ inches in diameter. The style-hole, filled with plaster, is 22 inches from the ground. There are two horizontal and two vertical lines, and in the west lower quadrant two lines, and in the east lower quadrant one line.

ST. MARTIN'S, SALISBURY, WILTS. Visited March 1923. One dial.

Dials on the walls of city churches seem to be very rare. This well-cut, large dial is on a buttress at the south-east corner of the chancel: it is one of two corner buttresses set at right angles to the walls, has two plain sloping set-offs, and is probably of thirteenth-century date. It faces S. 20° E., has no circle, but measures 9 inches from side to side. The style-hole is 46 inches from the ground, and the lines, thirteen in number, forming a complete half-wheel, are very evenly placed. In addition there is one other line just above the west horizontal line. (See Analysis, p. 125. Photo, Plate X.)

CHADDESLEY CORBETT, WORCS. Visited August 1922.
    Three dials.

There are three dials here, all on the south wall of the chancel, to the west of the priest's door. The wall faces S. 10° E.

1. The stone on which this dial appears is much weathered. The style-hole, 60 inches from the ground, is much damaged below and to the left. The dial has an irregular circle about 5 inches in diameter, but the lines measure $2\frac{1}{4}$ inches. There are two horizontal lines, and in the upper east quadrant are two indistinct lines. In the lower half there is a short (?) vertical line, and in the western quadrant a well-marked line which is nearer the horizontal than the (?) vertical line. In the lower eastern quadrant there are two lines.

2. The style-hole of this dial is in and below a horizontal joint and is 56 inches from the ground. It retains its broken-off style, which looks like iron. The joint forms the horizontal lines and there is nothing on the stone above. An indistinct part of a circle is seen on the western side. A vertical line and four others in the eastern quadrant are well cut, and in the western quadrant there are five faint lines. Radii measure $5\frac{3}{4}$ inches. (See Analysis, p. 115. Photo, Plate IV.)

3. This is an interesting and peculiar dial of a rare type. It is on the same wall as the two former. The style-hole, 74 inches from the ground, is in a vertical masonry joint which forms the vertical line of the dial,

but the horizontal lines seem to meet below the centre of the hole. There are no lines or circle in the upper half, but in the lower half there is an indistinct circle and thirteen lines numbered in Roman figures from VI to VI, the IV having four straight strokes and some of the figures being written backwards. The IX line is very well cut, and between the lines marked III and II there is an extra line with no number. (See Analysis, p. 116. Photo, Plate XII.)

To the west of these three dials is a fourteenth-century buttress with two gablets. Dial 3 is quite near this buttress. Dial 2 is next, and Dial 1 is farthest away. At the present time this buttress would prevent the sun in the late afternoon from casting a shadow on these dials, especially on Nos. 3 and 2. It would be interesting to know if the dials are *in situ* or if the buttress is a later addition.

HAMPTON LOVETT, WORCS. Visited May 1924. One dial.

This church, celebrated as the burial-place of the original of Sir Roger de Coverley, has a dial situated on an early Norman buttress on the south of the chancel. It consists of a style-hole, about 4 feet 3 inches from the ground, and a circle. The upper half of the latter is plain, but the lower half is divided into east and west quadrants by a vertical and two horizontal lines. The western quadrant has seven fairly distinct lines, but the eastern has been mutilated by deeply cut cross-lines.

HIMBLETON, WORCS. Visited August 10, 1922. A dial with numbered lines.

The dial here is most interesting and of a very unusual type ; it should be compared with the dial at Chaddesley Corbett in the same county. It is to be seen on a quoin at the east end of the south wall of the south transept, and there is a diagonal buttress on the corner below. Situated perhaps 15 or 20 feet from the ground, it has two concentric circles, and between these are the numbers XII, I, II, III, in Roman numerals. There are four lines starting from the style-hole and ending opposite the four figures. The vertical line, which here may with certainty be called the noon-line, is well marked and ends at the inner circle in a hole. The other three lines are in the right-hand lower quadrant. It seems impossible to avoid the conclusion that the numbers are meant to indicate the hours 12, 1, 2, and 3, and if this be granted, it follows that the style which threw a shadow at noon on the vertical line marked XII could not have projected from the face of the dial at *right angles*, for this dial faces 20° east of south, and, except on a dial facing due south, a style fixed at right angles does not give a vertical shadow at noon. On this dial, therefore, to obtain a vertical shadow at noon, the style must have been deflected 20° to the west, or, in other words, must have pointed due south. Fr. Horne mentions four dials with the lines numbered. (See sketch on p. 197.)

HOLT, WORCS. Visited August 14, 1922. Two dials.

Both these dials are on the south wall of the south aisle, a fourteenth-century wall, and to the west of a blocked doorway. They face due south. The stone is of soft material, and is much damaged by exposure to the weather. (Photo, Plate IV.)

1. The upper dial is 62 inches from the ground and has no circle. There are six lines, the vertical one being $1\frac{3}{4}$ inches long.

2. This dial has a complete circle, $3\frac{3}{4}$ inches in diameter, and is 50 inches from the ground. In the lower half there are four lines besides the two horizontal ones, and in the upper half two lines.

MARTLEY, WORCS. Visited September 1923. One dial.

The dial is on the south face of the south of two angular buttresses at the south-east corner of the chancel, probably a fourteenth-century buttress. The material is a soft red sandstone, and it has suffered much from exposure. The style-hole, which is very large, is surrounded by a circle which has no lines or holes in the upper half. In the lower half of the circle eleven holes and eight lines can be seen, some of the latter not reaching to the style-hole. The eastern lower quadrant is the most perfect, for here there are seven holes at regular intervals, showing that this was originally probably a half-wheel dial. (See Analysis, p. 129. Photo, Plate X.)

STOKE PRIOR, WORCS. Visited August 9, 1922. Two dials.

1. A dial on the south-west buttress of the nave, very much defaced. There is no circle and the large style-hole is about 100 inches from the ground. There are three lines in the lower half and two in the upper. It faces S. 15° E.

2. A dial on the tower, west of the priest's door, has a complete circle, 6 inches in diameter, and a large style-hole 85 inches from the ground. A well-marked vertical line, with two lines on each side of it, are visible and possibly there have been lines all round. The stone is much weathered. It faces S. 10° E.

STOULTON, WORCS. Visited May 1924. Three dials, and possibly one or two others.

1. This dial is on the west jamb of the south Norman doorway, and faces S. 14° W. The stone is blue lias and is covered with lichen. It is a very complicated dial and has no line forming a circle, but there are three

rings or portions of rings set at increasing distances from the style-hole and formed by small holes. It is difficult to describe accurately but—

The first ring of holes is 2 inches from the style-hole, is found only in the lower half of the dial, and is most distinct on the west side.

The second ring, formed of twenty-four holes, is 3½ inches from the style-hole and is complete all round.

The third ring is about 5 inches from the style-hole and is found only in the lowest part of the lower half.

Between the second and third rings, in the lower west quadrant, there are also a number of holes, perhaps two rows. These are about 4 inches from the style-hole.

In the lower half of the dial there are thirteen lines, nearly all perfect, which, as they radiate from the centre, cut through the holes which form the three rings mentioned above. There are also three imperfect lines in the upper eastern quadrant.

The style-hole, which is blocked, is 52 inches from the ground, which slopes considerably towards the wall. (Photo, Plate XI.)

2. On the same west jamb, below the first mentioned, is another dial. It is very indistinct, but radiating downwards from a well-marked style-hole are three or four lines with a part of a circle at the circumference.

3. On the east jamb of the same Norman doorway is a third dial. This faces S. 12° W. It has a style-hole 43 inches from the ground with a horizontal line on each side and a hole vertically below. It is 3¼ inches from this hole to the style-hole. In the lower western quadrant four lines can be seen, and faint traces of lines in the eastern quadrant.

TREDINGTON, WORCS. Visited April 4, 1925. One dial.

This church with its pre-Conquest windows and many

other interesting features, possesses one dial incised on the east jamb of the south doorway. This doorway dates from the twelfth century, but has been reset in the wall of a fourteenth-century aisle. The dial now faces due south, is about 7 feet from the ground, and its radii measure about 6 inches. It is an incomplete half-wheel dial, and part of a circle can be seen on the western side. Nine lines are visible.

WARNDON, WORCS. Visited May 1924. One dial.

This picturesque church with its half-timbered, black-and-white tower preserves one dial situated on a buttress (? fourteenth-century) on the south wall of the nave to the east of the south door. It is about 7 feet from the ground. The style-hole, which is blocked, presents the unusual feature of being square. There is no circle, but it measures 10 inches from side to side. There is a vertical line above and below the style-hole and a horizontal line on each side. Including the two horizontal ones, there are thirteen lines in the lower half, two of these being very faint. Parts of two other lines can be seen in the left upper quadrant. Some of the lines appear to have been rescraped recently. It faces S. 12° E.

LIST OF CHURCHES NOT DESCRIBED ABOVE WHERE DIALS HAVE BEEN FOUND BY THE AUTHOR

Bredon, Worcs.   One on buttress on south of chancel.
Overbury, Worcs.   Seven, near priest's door.
Eckington, Worcs.   One, near priest's door.
Burford, Oxon.   One, near priest's door.
Wyck Rissington, Glos.   One, near priest's door.
     Doubtful.
Oddington, Glos.   One, on south porch.
Bledington, Glos.   One, on south porch.

Icomb, Glos. One, on south porch.

Lower Swell, Glos. Two, east of porch.

Northleach, Glos. One, on a south buttress.

Coln St. Denis, Glos. One, on a south buttress.

Coln Rogers, Glos. One, on pilaster strip on south of nave.

Bibury, Glos. One, on south porch. Very good one.

Coln St. Aldwyn, Glos. One, on a buttress of the tower.

Quenington, Glos. One, on south Norman buttress.

Fairford, Glos. One, on a south buttress.

Down Ampney, Glos. Two, on tower buttresses.

Maisey Hampton, Glos. Six—three on south transept and three on south porch.

Ampney St. Mary, Glos. One, on buttress.

Ampney St. Peter, Glos. One, on north-west buttress of tower.

Ampney Crucis, Glos. One, on south porch.

Daglingworth, Glos. One, on buttress. Also a Saxon dial.

Dymock, Glos. One, on Norman buttress at south-east corner of nave.

Inglesham, Glos. One, on sculpture of Virgin and Child, now in the church.

Aylton, Hereford. One.

Ledbury, Hereford. Two, on a buttress of south aisle.

Burcombe, Wilts. One, on south-east angle of chancel.

Brabourne, Kent. Two, on south doorway.

Saxon Sundials

Warnford, Hants. Visited August 11, 1923.

Corhampton, Hants. Visited June 7, 1922.

Winchester St. Michael's, Hants.

Daglingworth, Glos. Visited May 1920.

Castle Froome, Hereford.   Visited March 1921.
Arreton, Isle of Wight.   (?) Visited October, 1925.

The lists which are here given, for convenience of
reference, contain dials showing some special feature
or some abnormality.

1. *Inverted or Upside-down Dials*

Baughurst Nos. 1 and 2.   (See p. 143 and Plates XII
   and II.)
Herriard No. 8.   (See p. 157.)
Stockbridge.   (See p. 173.)
Winchfield Nos. 1 and 2.   (See p. 179 and Plate XV.)

2. *Dials in Abnormal Positions*

Ashe.   Now faces north.   (P. 142.)
Baughurst Nos. 1 and 2.   Now both face west.   (P. 142.)
Laverstoke No. 1.   Now faces north.   (P. 162.)
Laverstoke No. 2.   Faces east.   (P. 163.)
Sherborne St. John No. 5.   Faces east.   (P. 171.)
Steventon No. 1.   Now faces west.   (P. 172.)
Stockbridge.   Now faces west.   (P. 173.)
Martin Nos. 1 and 2.   Face S. 35° W.   (P. 163.)
Martin No. 3.   Faces S. 36° E.   (P. 164.)
N. Hayling.   Situated on the set-off of a buttress and
   faces somewhat upwards.   (P. 153.)
Newton Valence.   Both dials are now covered by a
   modern vestry.   (P. 165.)
Preston Candover.   Is now level with the ground.
   (P. 166.)
Soberton.   Faces east.   A doubtful dial.   (P. 171.)

Dials having a line marked with a +

Baughurst No. 2.   (P. 143 and Plate II.)
Sherborne St. John No. 3.   (P. 170 and Plate XV.)

Dials the lines of which are marked with Roman numerals

Chaddesley Corbett No. 3. (P. 189 and Plate XII.)
Himbleton. (P. 190 and sketch on this page.)

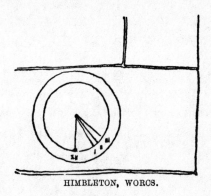

HIMBLETON, WORCS.

Dials which retain the broken-off stump of the gnomon

Laverstoke No. 1. Iron. (P. 162.)
Newton Valence No. 2. (?) Iron. (P. 165.)
Warblington. Soft white metal. (P. 177.)
Chaddesley Corbett No. 2. (?) Iron. (P. 189.)
Brockenhurst. (?) Iron. (P. 146.)
Arreton, Isle of Wight. Metal. (P. 180.)

Dials with wedge-shaped lines

Sherborne St. John No. 4. (P. 170.)
Upham. (P. 176 and Plate XIV.)
Barfreston No. 3. (P. 185 and Plate I.)

Dials with square style-hole

Warndon. (P. 194.)
Downton. (P. 187 and Plate V.)
Newton Valence. (P. 165.)

INDEX TO TEXT AND ILLUSTRATIONS

Note.—The churches printed in black type are those on which the Author has found one or more Mass-clocks.

The letter A before a number indicates that the analysis of the dial is on that page.

The letter D before a number indicates that the description of the dial is on that page.

The numbers in black type indicate the important references.

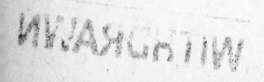